Beyond Human Scale

BEYOND
HUMAN SCALE

The Large Corporation
at Risk

ELI GINZBERG

AND

GEORGE VOJTA

Basic Books, Inc., Publishers   New York

Library of Congress Cataloging in Publication Data
Ginzberg, Eli
    Beyond human scale.
    Includes index.
    1. Executives—United States. 2. Corporations—
United States. 3. Employee morale—United States.
4. Personnel management—United States. I. Vojta,
George. II. Title.
HD38.25.U6G59 1985   658.4   84–45317
ISBN 0–465–00658–2

CONTENTS

Contents

PART IV
Resolutions

PREFACE

The reader may be interested in the answers to the following three questions: How did an older professor of economics happen to collaborate with a younger banker in writing this book? What was the nature of the collaboration? And how can their analysis and conclusions be assessed?

Their collaboration predates the present effort and goes back to the late 1970s when George Vojta was Executive Vice President for Strategic Planning at Citicorp and, as a part of the bank's reassessment of national and international economic and urban trends, sought the assistance of Eli Ginzberg and the members of the staff of the Conservation of Human Resources, Columbia University, which he directs. That collaboration focused on the growth of the service economy, and led to two publications: an article by Ginzberg and Vojta in *Scientific American* (March 1981) on "The Service Sector of the U.S. Economy," and a book by Thomas Stanback, Jr., and his colleagues on *Services: The New Economy.*

One by-product of the collaboration was to call our attention to the growth of the large corporation in many service industries, and the corresponding greater reliance of these firms on college-educated personnel. We became aware of important tensions between corporate scale and the preferences and performance of managerial personnel and decided that this theme was worth more attention than it had previously attracted.

Moreover, in reflecting on his half century of experience with large organizations, which involved extended consulting with major federal government agencies and with leading U.S. multinationals, Ginzberg had long been impressed with the non-fit between corporate structures and the work of their middle- and higher-level managers. Vojta, in turn, had intimate knowledge of the human resources system of one of the nation's premiere corporations, further refined by his consulting assignments at home and abroad.

Drawing on our respective experiences we began a dialogue aimed at identifying, analyzing, and synthesizing the key issues that define the interaction between large organizational structures and how their managers carry out their work and pursue their career goals. The dialogue was intense; it went on for three years; and in the process we produced reams of memoranda aimed at sharpening our understanding of the dynamics of the interaction between scale and people. In the spring of 1984 we had a publishable manuscript.

The third question relates to the nature of our evidence and the validity of our analysis and conclusions. The principal source of our "data" was a combined total of three-quarters of a century of participant observation in large organizations and corporations, aided and abetted by the prior studies of many scholars and contemporary analysts, and further informed by several hundred conversations, mostly informal, with knowledgeable persons who had firsthand exposure to the problems forming the heart of this inquiry.

The answer to the question of how the validity of our formulation can be assessed is relatively simple: those with first-hand knowledge of the ways of life in a large corporation must check what we say against their own experiences. They, and they alone, are in a position to assess this work, and we are comfortable that they are a jury of our peers.

ELI GINZBERG
GEORGE VOJTA
September 1984

ACKNOWLEDGMENTS

Dr. Dean Morse, who has been for many years a Senior Research Associate of the Conservation of Human Resources Project at Columbia University, played a major supportive role at every stage of this work. He joined us during our initial planning; he helped to sharpen our approach; he ferreted out obscure literature that contained valuable leads; he criticized and improved our formulations at each stage of their evolution; he read and corrected successive drafts of the manuscript. He did all of the above and more with unfailing good nature and friendliness.

Ruth S. Ginzberg used her light editorial pencil, and the authors are pleased to acknowledge her help.

Sylvia Leef and Shoshana Vasheetz helped to reproduce and kept excellent control over the successive drafts of the manuscript, for which we are in their debt.

Martin Kessler, our publisher and editor, made a great number of constructive suggestions. Sheila Friedling oversaw the copy editing and in the process made our text more readable.

PART I

Overview

Introduction

This book is about the large corporation and how it uses its human resources, particularly its managerial personnel. It is our thesis that the increasing scale and complexity of the large corporation results in the underutilization of its managerial personnel, with adverse effects not only on morale and performance but ultimately on growth and profitability as well. This is no trivial matter. Since the large corporation is the dominant business institution in the United States and other advanced economies, its growing difficulties in effectively utilizing its managerial personnel must have a negative impact on both economic performance and societal development, not to mention the well-being and satisfaction of its managers.

A 1983 survey undertaken by the American Management Association and written up as *Middle Management Morale in the Eighties* by George Edward Breen concludes that "collectively, the middle managers in our survey cast a strong vote of 'no confidence' in their current corporate leadership, both in its ability to guide their organizations through the troubled eighties and in its efforts to prepare them for individual career advancement." These findings may indeed startle top managers, who also were rated well below par in their basic "honesty and straightforwardness." In fact, only 33 percent of the respondents agreed with the statement, "Middle managers in my organization respect the honesty and straightforwardness of top management."

The authors of the survey report had anticipated that managers might complain about their salaries, their working conditions, or their promotional opportunities. But their negative assessment of corporate leadership was unexpected, and it clearly signals pervasive dissatisfaction and low morale among a significant segment of middle managers.

We believe that this issue of low morale in the managerial hierarchy calls for attention, analysis, and correction. But first we must acknowledge its larger social context: since Vietnam and Watergate, we have seen Americans express loss of confidence in most of our key institutions. The Harris Survey of November 1983, for example, tabulates the decline since 1966 in "Confidence in Institutions" in terms of the percentage of respondents who expressed a "great deal of confidence":

	1966 (%)	1983 (%)
Colleges and Universities	61	36
The Military	61	35
Medicine	73	35
The U.S. Supreme Court	50	33
The White House	—	23
Organized Religion	41	22
Major Companies	55	18
Organized Labor	22	10

SOURCE: From "Confidence in Institutions Survey," Louis Harris and Associates, November 1983.

The total list comprises fourteen institutions. It is worth noting that of these institutions, major companies are third from the bottom. In seeking the source of this low level of confidence, our inquiry will trace the development of the organizational structures and decision-making processes used by large corporations to cope with the scale and complexity of their operations.

Introduction

This development has much to teach us about the dysfunctional impact of size and structure on the utilization of people at all levels of management, from the executive trainee to the chief executive. The scaffolding to support this analysis contains several segments.

But for the main explanation for low morale among managers we must turn to the corporation itself. In chapter 1 we present our thesis that the structure of the large corporation has created a poor working environment, impeding the effective use of the energies, talents, and leadership of its managers.

In part II, *Perspectives,* to gain some initial insight into the problem, we look at four highly relevant topics: large organizations that are not organized for profit; economists' treatment—or, rather, nontreatment—of the large corporation; the rapid growth of the large corporation in the half century after 1920 and the increasing difficulties it is encountering in today's world of heightened volatility; and the significant changes that have occurred in our nation's manpower pool.

These comparative, economic, historical, and human resources perspectives are each useful in different ways. We found, for instance, that even in the absence of a money-making objective, large organizations with a military, religious, or eleemosynary goal are beset with many of the same difficulties that large corporations face in deploying their managerial personnel effectively and coping with changes in their environment.

A scanning of the works of leading economists reveals that most of them have focused almost exclusively on the operations of the competitive market. Economists have had little to say on the large corporation and how it uses its managerial personnel and reaches decisions, key processes that over time will determine its growth and profitability. A look at the historical record suggests that the large corporation was well adapted to the environment of rapid growth that characterized the U.S. economy throughout most of the half century after 1920. More recently, heightened environmental volatility and changes in the expectations of its managerial personnel have brought the corporation under increasing pressure.

Our final perspective reveals a work force that differs strikingly from those of earlier periods in gender, ethnic and racial composition, age, educational preparation, and career expectations. Adjusting to these human resources changes is a major challenge to corporate management, a challenge that it has only begun to recognize.

In part III, *Scale and Managers,* the analysis turns inward. We look at the ways in which the large corporation has sought to cope with increasing scale by modifying its structure and at the consequences of such evolving structures for decision making, the use of managerial personnel, and long-term viability and profitability.

Separate chapters are devoted to two different adverse consequences of the scale and structure of large organizations: the underutilization of managerial personnel and the excessive demands that are placed on the chief executives who are responsible for current operations as well as the future positioning of their enterprises. Part III then concludes with a human resources agenda focusing on the ways that large organizations can reorganize to make more effective use of their managerial talent.

In the final chapter of this book, we look to the future and explore the changing national and world environments within which the large corporation must operate if it is to create a better setting for the work of its managers and if it is to respond successfully to new external challenges and opportunities. One conclusion is unequivocal: only those large corporations that learn to use their managerial personnel effectively in the increasingly competitive world economy will survive and prosper.

1

The Thesis

The main thesis of this book can be simply stated: The large corporation, because of the way it is organized, forces managers to spend much of their time and energy preparing reports for supervisors, coordinating with other managers, and protecting their turf so that in countless ways they are constrained from using their own initiative.

The skeptic will argue that this pessimistic view cannot possibly be correct since large corporations dominate the economies of all advanced nations in Europe, North America, and the Far East. Clearly there is a contradiction between their leadership role and this critical judgment.

Before confronting this paradox, we should point out that our inquiry gave us many opportunities to discuss our thesis with business executives at all levels of the corporate hierarchy. Two examples will illustrate the responses we received. On a recent trip to Europe, the senior writer encountered a former student who remarked in passing that he was currently the half-owner of an export-import business and was getting ready to buy the rest. In response to the comment that he must have had his fill of working for a large corporation, he exploded, "You bet! After eleven years with [a major electronics concern], I couldn't wait to get out." A recently retired chief executive of one of the nation's leading industrial concerns remarked: "There's no doubt that most large companies are overstructured. After I took over, I ran the place without an organizational chart for five years."

For the most part we encountered quick comprehension and broad acceptance of the linkage we make between the structure of large corporations and their ineffective use of human resources. Since those most knowledgeable about the working environment of large corporations confirmed our thesis, there indeed seems to be a contradiction between the problems of the corporate environment and the reality of the dominance and success of large corporations.

But this contradiction can be explained if we distinguish between the success of the species—large corporations as a collective body—and the vitality, profitability, and survival of any specific large corporation. Consider, by analogy, the long dominance of the nation-state, whose origins can be traced back to antiquity, and the many examples of the once powerful nations that have declined and, in most cases, disappeared.

Although the large corporation has had pretentions to immortality ever since it was no longer dependent on any one individual as leader, the incontrovertible fact is that within as short a period as sixty years, there has been considerable turnover in leadership. If we look at listings by *Forbes* of the largest U.S. industrial corporations in 1917 and 1977, we find only one corporation (Exxon, the largest unit of the old Standard Oil trust) in the top ten of both lists. Four of the earlier top ten have disappeared through merger (Armour, Swift, Midvale Steel and Ordnance, and U.S. Rubber), and three others are currently in trouble (U.S. Steel, Bethlehem, International Harvester). The remaining two (DuPont and GE) have slipped into a lower bracket.

Fortune in its issue of May 5, 1980 produced a twenty-five-year comparative analysis of the companies included in its 500 list. The turnover of companies is even more startling, since the period is briefer and was for the most part characterized by strong economic expansion at home and abroad. Of those

The Thesis

companies on the list in 1955, only 262, or slightly more than half, were still on the list in 1980; 147 on the later list had been too small to make the original list and another 91 had been privately held, had not been in existence, or had not been previously classified as industrial companies.

The essence of our thesis is reflected in a feature article in the *Wall Street Journal* (January 27, 1984) on the turnaround of Bank America Corporation, the second largest bank-holding company in the United States. Samuel Armacost, the recently installed president who has the task of energizing the "sleeping giant," has focused in large part on human resources and corporate structure. As the article states, he "inherited an institution whose top management ranks were thin and whose middle management was peopled largely by complacent bureaucrats ill-suited for a deregulated banking industry." Armacost quickly decided to close 150 of the more than 1,000 California branches and eliminate between 4,000 and 8,000 jobs. His personnel chief, hired from IBM, aimed at "injecting entrepreneurial spirit into Bank America's sluggish bureaucracy, which many say is afflicted with turf wars and battles between the old guard and the new. Many in the bank's work force of 80,000 compare its old personnel policies to the civil service. Everybody at a certain grade could expect about the same salary and the same increase. ... No longer. Exceptional employees are publicly showered with recognition—and cash.... We're trying to drive a wedge between our top performers and our non-performers."

The Importance of Human Resources Utilization

There are a number of reasons for our decision to concentrate on the impact of corporate organizational structure on human resources utilization in appraising the present performance and future prospects of the large corporation. To begin with, those economists who have played a leading role in studying the evolution of modern industrial societies have largely neglected the internal operations of the corporation. They have centered their attention on transactions in the marketplace, where competing producers vie with one another to attract purchasers who are seeking the best buys at the lowest price. The competitive theory on which they rely to explain the behavior of businessmen is predicated on the simplifying assumption that all of them seek to maximize their profits within acceptable parameters of risk. They ascribe to the large corporation the patterns of decision making and market behavior that earlier economists derived from their studies of the small businessman.

We, however, do not believe that this extrapolation is justified because a large corporation differs in many respects from a small business owned and managed by one individual. In the small organization, power is highly concentrated; in the large organization, it is inevitably diffuse, a basic difference which has major implications for managerial behavior and organizational efficiency.

A second reason for focusing on the human resources dimension of the large corporation has to do with the increasing importance of human resources in modern advanced economies. Today, wages, salaries, fringe benefits, and the labor component of the self-employed together account for over 80 percent of all national income. Returns to capital account for under 20 percent. We continue to call ours a capitalist economy but a more descriptive term would be a "human economy" since it is human resources that dominate all economic activity, from the research laboratory to retailing. Significantly, a former chief executive of Bloomingdale's, the New York City department store, once remarked that the only barrier to doubling the store's sales was his inability to hire and retain competent salespersons.

And there are other reasons for focusing on human resources. In a large corporation, as in a small one, all that transpires is the result of prior and current decision making that is centered

The Thesis

in the managerial cadre, particularly in senior managers. The effectiveness with which managers reach and implement decisions has a determining influence on the profitability, growth, and survival of the business enterprise. As the number of decision makers increases, the process becomes more complex and there is more room for slippage. As we will discuss later, there are many advantages to scale, but the number of managers involved in corporate decision making is not one of them.

One of the strengths of every large organization is its ability to establish policies and procedures informed by its successes in the past. Thus, new additions to the ranks of management are indoctrinated in the company's way of responding to new situations. This saves them from having to develop their own answers and insures adherence to company policy.

However, the value of such distilled experience as a guide for decision making diminishes once important discontinuities occur in the markets in which the corporation is active. The increasing volatility that has characterized the world's economy since the mid-1960s—the high level of inflation, the oil crisis, disturbed financial markets, long-term recession, and debt moratoria—requires that all economic agents modify their traditional ways of acting and reacting. Such volatility requires innovative and speedy decision making, a requirement that the large corporation has difficulty in meeting by virtue of its history, its large number of managers, and its formal decision-making mechanisms. The Boston Consulting Group ended its insightful commentary on "Beyond Portfolios" (1984) with the following statement: "Large portions of the economic landscape are no longer hospitable to major corporate enterprise."

One further development reinforces our emphasis on the role of human resources in the large corporation. Today a significant proportion of the young people who find their way into the managerial ranks complete four years of college and two years of additional professional education. During these years they must be supported by their parents, take out loans, and/or seek to earn part of their expenses, which in total may amount to $100,000 for these six years of higher education. Nor does this sizable sum take into account what economists refer to as "income foregone," that is, the income students could have earned had they held regular jobs instead.

Clearly, the large numbers of young people who make such substantial investments in their education develop certain aspirations and expectations about their careers, which will exercise a shaping influence on their future behavior. We doubt that most large corporations have devoted adequate attention to this change in the values and goals of their junior and middle managers. And yet only by doing so will they establish a working environment in which they can effectively utilize their managerial personnel.

Dr. Douglas W. Bray, the director of human resources research for AT&T prior to its recent breakup, sought to alert his superiors in the late 1970s to the striking changes that he had uncovered between the generation of managers who entered the company shortly after World War II and the more recent arrivals. On the basis of elaborate testing, measurements, and attitude surveys, Bray concluded that the more recent management trainees were less inclined to claw and fight their way up the corporate hierarchy. Their personal goals did not center to nearly the same extent as their predecessors' on achieving a position of authority and responsibility where they could manage and control the work of large numbers of subordinates. Rather, their primary aim was to pursue a life-style that would provide them with interpersonal satisfactions based on close relations to people of their own choosing. Power, prestige, and money were much lower on their value scales.

What does this mean for the future of the large corporation, which up to now has been able to function by relying on a complex organizational structure staffed by layers of well-educated managers? Today many of the managers find that the structures within which they have to function make inadequate use of their knowledge and potential and, further, fail to fulfill some of their other expectations. Moreover, recent cohorts of young managers are not as determined as their predecessors to fight their way up the corporate hierarchy. And all this is happening at a time when the markets in which large corporations compete are becoming increasingly volatile so that there is increasing pressure to improve corporate decision-making mechanisms. It is our view that many large corporations are at risk precisely because of their underutilization of managerial personnel.

Let us try to sketch the analytic framework that we will use to explore how, and with what consequences, corporate structure impacts on managerial performance. The large corporation usually comes into being because it has established a niche for itself through an innovation in product, process, or marketing that has enabled it to grow rapidly and to earn profits with which to finance part or all of its expansion. The most successful small corporations become large corporations by producing a new or improved product that the market wants in large quantities for an extended period of time. Such a conjuncture is not easy to achieve, but when a small enterprise succeeds in producing something that the market wants, and that other corporations cannot match, it is on its way to becoming a large corporation.

While the concept of the niche has been central to the analysis of the business enterprise, the concomitant concept of the "cushion" has often been neglected. Yet the cushion, as we shall see, crucially affects managerial decision making in large organizations.

The "Cushion"

The cushion, which represents in large measure the accumulation of retained profits, helps to establish and maintain the atmosphere of security and long-range optimism that characterizes most large corporations. This cushion provides constant reassurance to top and middle management that the corporation has proved itself in the marketplace and that it can face the present and the future with confidence. All levels of the organization, from the CEO to the executive trainee, believe that the corporation is free to move largely under its own momentum.

The cushion also gives top management considerable discretion in responding to a declining market or meeting and surmounting unexpected challenges. The 1980–1982 recession forced a large number of leading U.S. corporations to reassess their long-term strategy and take radical actions to improve their profitability. A significant number found it expedient to "sell off" units that were no longer contributing an appropriate share to total corporate profits and growth. Often, however, these divestitures were preceded by long delays before the final decision, delays that frequently reflected top management's procrastination based on hopes of a favorable turn in the market. Senior executives generally seek to avoid downscaling the assets on their balance sheet, since such a move signals the securities markets that a significant write-down has occurred. Robert Townsend in *Further Up the Organization* (1984) describes his difficulty in getting the owners to shut down a losing division that was on the way to sinking the company. He kept calling them up with his most recent estimate of how long it would be before insolvency. With a week to go, the owners finally took action.

An investment banker who specializes in the rehabilitation of corporations headed for (or already in) bankruptcy insists that the danger signs are always present years earlier but that management and the board tend to ignore them. In his view, no company collapses as the result of a single shock; it collapses only from repeated failures to take corrective actions.

There is ample evidence for this view. To give just one example, on April 5, 1984, the *New York Times* ran a front-page story entitled "Losses Lead RCA to Cancel Videodisk Player Production"—a product it had once dubbed the company's

The Thesis

"Manhattan Project." RCA's pretax losses on the product totaled $114 million in 1981, $107 million in 1982, $110 million in 1983, and $17 million in the first quarter of 1984. Thornton F. Bradshaw, chairman and chief executive of RCA, said: "We took the decision with obvious disappointment in the face of continuing losses and narrowing prospects that the business would ever turn profitable." The company's major mistake, according to Bradshaw, "was in not seeing what the market would do." The sharp drop in the price of videocassette recorders and the consumer preference to rent movies for a few dollars a night had doomed the videodisk player.

On occasion, the exercise of deliberate speed in divestitures may be a sign of sound business judgment, not managerial timidity. For example, when a large pharmaceutical company recently reached a firm decision to spin off a number of units, it was determined to find an attractive buyer for the first unit so as to signal its managers that their career interests were being taken into account. Top management was concerned that unless it reassured those middle managers whom it wanted to retain, many would leave.

But there can be many reasons, beyond the disinclination of top management to take action that may reflect unfavorably on its financial stewardship, for management's deciding—aided by its cushion—to delay a divestiture. It is not easy for a CEO to cut loose a major division, which often means breaking an employment relationship with associates, many of whom he views as competent. And if he himself spent a considerable part of his career in the failing division, he may be even more hesitant to act since his ties would be deeper and his commitments stronger. In one large insurance company, the CEO dragged his feet for years because the unprofitable division had been the base from which his own corporate career had been launched. When he could no longer avoid a decision, he placed a new manager in charge of the unit and announced that at the end of the year he would take definitive action either to retain and rebuild or spin off the unit, depending on the advice of the new division head. He finally had to do something, and this solution offered him the best way out.

The importance of the cushion in enabling large corporations to survive despite major setbacks is underscored by the case of AT&T, which reported a $4.9 billion loss in the fourth quarter of 1983, explained in large measure by the write-down of assets coincident to the breakup of the system. The previous largest quarterly loss of any U.S. corporation was reported by Bethlehem Steel for the last three months of 1982, during which it lost $1.15 billion.

The cushion is important not only because it enables top management to minimize poor performance in one or more divisions or in the corporation as a whole, but also because it provides opportunities to speed (or sometimes to delay) growth by merger and acquisition. Often these additions do lead to improvements in its balance sheet by enhanced cash flow and additional earnings. But time must pass before it can be concluded that the new unit or units have in fact strengthened the parent company. In many instances, the passage of time does not substantiate the earlier optimistic conclusion. The existence of a large cushion can work in either of two directions: to speed the corporation's adaptation to change or to slow its response. Often it has the second effect.

The cushion also influences the attitudes and behavior of middle management. The existence of the cushion creates an environment in which middle managers are under less pressure to keep their attention riveted on the market and the competition. The cushion makes it much easier for managers to look inward, and it encourages them to pursue the corporate power game since they feel secure in their jobs and in the corporation's future.

Economies of scale contribute to the growth and profitability of the large corporation. The large corporation can often manufacture, distribute, and finance at a unit cost below what it

The Thesis

would have to pay in the marketplace. In the opinion of Professor Oliver Williamson of Yale, a leading student of corporate enterprise, the engine that drives the large corporation to further growth and profitability is precisely this ability to save "transaction costs" by accomplishing functions internally rather than relying on the market.

The Management Information System (MIS)

The more the large corporation depends on itself, the greater its need for a system of internal accounts that will enable it to monitor the performance of its various divisions and of the company as a whole. It may be a year before a part bought by one division finds its way through a number of other divisions into a machine that is sold to a customer. A company must maintain control over its costs during such a long production cycle. In new product development, a period of several years may pass between initial developmental outlays and the first sales in the market. For example, a *Fortune* article (April 30, 1984) reported on the efforts that Richard Mahoney and his senior team are making to assure the future of Monsanto by investing heavily in research directed toward new product innovation in the mid-1990s.

Those at the top of the corporation need data and information about how well or poorly the principal divisions of the company are performing so that they can decide whether to make corrections in course. At the beginning of each budget cycle, agreements are reached between those at the top and those with operating responsibility in the line divisions about objectives and goals, all geared to a timetable. The principal internal system of control that is relied upon for the critical data is the management information system (MIS).

One of modern physics' great achievements was to demonstrate that the instruments used to measure the behavior of natural phenomena influence the results. The researcher cannot completely eliminate the distortions introduced by the instruments he employs. A parallel difficulty has been noted in other areas of measurement. After decades of research into the measurement of intelligence, many believe that intelligence can best be defined in terms of the scores that individuals achieve on IQ tests. But the question remains moot because the experts cannot agree on how to construct valid tests.

It is not surprising that there are difficulties in designing an MIS, which reflects the performances of the several subdivisions of a large corporation. As with any information-gathering and control system, distortions are inevitable. The officials in top management responsible for managing the MIS must resort to subjective judgment in allocating overhead among the principal profit centers, in establishing transfer prices for products moving between divisions, in determining an internal cost for capital, and, in some instances, in allocating revenues from final sales.

But why should the presence of subjective elements in the structuring and operation of an MIS have adverse effects on managerial performance? The performance of profit-center managers is judged by how well they meet or exceed the goals and targets which have been set and to which they have agreed. As a result, some managers may see an advantage in negotiating with the guardians of the MIS for a reduction in overhead costs allocated to their center. If they succeed in these negotiations, their performance results may be substantially improved, with corresponding gains to themselves in bonuses and reputation.

It is of course eminently sensible for the individual manager to invest time and effort in such negotiations since even modest adjustments can often have a significant impact on his final results. But there is little or no profit to the corporation as a whole.

The Thesis

The Performance Appraisal System

In addition to the MIS, all large corporations resort to another measurement device, the performance appraisal system, which enables them to assess the accomplishment of each person on the managerial hierarchy from the beginner to the chief executive. With thousands of managers assigned to different positions, many of them stationed far from corporate headquarters, it is essential that those at the top have a system in place for assessing the performance of all persons on the managerial ladder. In turn, those who are seeking to make their way up the hierarchy need information about their work and future prospects beyond that provided by periodic salary adjustments and promotions; they need to know how their work is viewed by their superiors and how they might improve their performance.

The performance appraisal system facilitates the delegation of authority and responsibility down the line and helps to assure that the assigned work will be effectively performed. Each manager knows that his or her immediate supervisor and, in most instances, the supervisor's boss will annually, or even every six months, review and make a permanent record of their appraisals of the manager's performance, on the basis of which future changes in his or her salary and position will be made. The performance appraisal system creates the glue that enables a highly structured corporation dependent on specialized work assignments to function.

An appraisal system used by management to assess the performance capabilities and potential of all persons in its executive ranks powerfully influences how effectively the corporation deploys its human resources. But as is true of all systems, performance appraisals have limitations and defects that distort outcomes. Since we will deal at length with performance appraisals at a later point (chapter 9), we need go no further here than to call attention to a few of the inherent weaknesses of this system.

The first point is that the individual or individuals who make the appraisals, especially immediate supervisors, are never free from conflict. Subordinates and supervisors are to some degree in competition with each other, if not now then perhaps some time in the future. Even leaving this competitive factor aside, many subjective considerations are likely to intervene, if for no other reason than that, to a large extent, performance appraisal systems focus on assessing a wide range of factors that cannot be objectively determined or quantified. The following traits have been rated as "personal qualities that are generally admired in the work place." *Responsible* and *honest* received ratings in the 80 to 90 percent range; *capable,* in the 60s; *imaginative, logical, ambitious,* and *broadminded,* in the 30 to 50 percent range; and *self-controlled, independent, helpful, intellectual, cheerful, courageous,* and *loving* in the 15 to 30 percent range. The elusive, nonobjective nature of these traits indicates how fragile are managerial appraisals based on such criteria.

This listing of desirable work qualities is extracted from a recent study (1982) by the American Management Association on *Managerial Values and Expectations.* The report also noted that in the case of ratings by peers, superiors, and subordinates, the trait of "competency" was identified by no more than 17 percent of the respondents. Such traits as integrity, leadership, and cooperation together accounted for 50 percent or more.

Further difficulties arise out of operational realities. A supervisor will hesitate to mark an employee "unsatisfactory" if he thus initiates a personnel review that could eventually result in the employee's dismissal. Moreover, he will probably have to defend this rating, and if his superiors do not sustain his judgment, he will lose standing with them.

Every supervisor recognizes that his evaluation and the feedback he provides to the person assessed will affect the latter's future work, attitudes, and behavior. Many supervisors trim their evaluations to this reality. In turn, many subordinates go out of their way to be agreeable to their supervisors because they believe that they will gain more from such behavior than they would by concentrating on their work performance.

Divisionalization

The fourth factor that leads to the underutilization of managerial personnel in the large corporation is the presence of a number of major subsidiary units. Top management must delegate power and responsibility to such units, to obtain the benefits of decentralization and divisionalization and to lessen its own involvement in day-to-day operations. But such gains come at a cost. By delegating authority and responsibility, the large corporation is transformed in reality, if not in law, into an association of cooperating but also competing units. Once divisions are established and then encouraged to increase their market share and profits, they see things from their vantage point—that is, in terms of what they know and what will be advantageous to them. Their perspective may be quite different from that of top executives, who have an overview of the corporation as a whole. And while top executives (with the support of the board of directors) retain the power to reorganize the corporation and even to sell it, they cannot ignore the potential costs of seeking to reduce or shift power previously allocated to subsidiary managers. Any such move is risky since corporate performance depends to a great extent on the effectiveness with which subsidiary managers carry out their assignments. Thus, top managements seek to avoid power conflicts with subsidiary managers or to moderate them when they arise.

It is understandable that most economists in analyzing the large corporation continue to use their time-honored assumption of profit-maximizing behavior. But that is a crude oversimplification of the environment within a large multidivisional corporation, where top management is constantly under conflicting pressures from its major units.

The phrase "NIH"—"not invented here"—indicates the determination of powerful units in a large organization to go their own way, pushing their own strategies, ideas, and products, and avoiding assistance from other divisions. To neglect the constant struggles among subsidiary units of large corporations for more resources and power—as well as for protecting what they have—is to overlook an important aspect of the internal dynamics of such organizations, one that has a determining effect on the behavior of middle and senior managers. Indeed, in many corporations, top management encourages such interdivisional competition in the belief that it contributes to managerial effectiveness and performance.

The CEO

The last major factor we must consider is the role of the chief executive officer (CEO). What impact does the CEO have on the utilization of managerial talent and on overall corporate performance? By law, contract, and tradition the CEO in the United States has wide-ranging powers and responsibility. The board of directors holds the CEO responsible for all aspects of corporate performance, current operating results as well as long-term corporate growth and profitability. Some years ago when the U.S. Department of Justice won a criminal case against senior executives in the electrical manufacturing industry, resulting in jail sentences for several, the CEO of General Electric insisted that he had no previous knowledge of the behavior of his subordinates and that they had acted in direct violation of written company policy. But Mark Cresap, the CEO of Westinghouse, was closer to the mark when he stated that as the head of his company, he could not avoid responsibility for the behavior of his subordinates.

Many CEOs are in office long enough to play a key role in the selection of their boards of directors. This, of course, adds to their control and domination of the corporation. Moreover, if the corporation has done well under his leadership, a strong CEO is likely to exercise major influence on the selection of his successor. Many boards believe that it would be foolish not to follow the advice of a successful retiring CEO; they just assume that he is in the best position to judge the strengths and weaknesses of the key contenders for his position. But this assumption may be contrary to fact. Consider the demonstrated lack of enthusiasm that President Eisenhower revealed on several occasions for his vice-president. Surely Eisenhower's attitude had much to do with Nixon's defeat in 1960. Again, consider the short leash on which President Johnson held his vice-president, Hubert Humphrey, refusing to allow him to distance himself from the unpopular war in Vietnam. Johnson may well have cost Humphrey the election in 1968. Strong men often prefer weak associates; and heightened emotional factors, which are likely to accompany approaching retirement, also affect the choice of a successor.

Scattered evidence suggests that in recent years the terms of CEOs of large corporations have been reduced to less than one decade. Since alignments among senior executives tend to form in advance, sometimes several years in advance, of a CEO's retirement, a considerable number of early retirements, resignations, and reassignments often follow the appointment of a new CEO. All this can have a significant impact on corporate performance. If a CEO encounters difficulties that force him out of office before his expected retirement date, the impact will be that much greater. In less than a decade, RCA has had four chief executives. Admittedly, this was an atypical situation, but it was surely a major factor in the mediocre record of the company until its recent stabilization and improvement.

But the heart of the problem lies in the way organizational structure and the corporate decision-making process compound the difficulties that the CEO faces in discharging his broad range of responsibilities. The man at the top needs current and correct information; he needs early warnings about emerging problems and the malperformance of key subordinates. Yet organizational structure and corporate folkways often militate against his receiving the warnings he needs to take corrective action in time.

A critical task of every CEO is to moderate and contain wasteful competition among major divisions and also between staff and line. An organization plagued by internal turmoil cannot respond successfully to threats and opportunities in the marketplace. The greater the congeniality among senior executives, the less time and effort are wasted in wrangling and later smoothing over hurt feelings. Exxon, in former days, relied exclusively on internal directors. Since they had to work together day in and day out, it was board procedure that if a decision did not command unanimous agreement, it would be tabled for subsequent action.

Of course, there is a danger that peace and harmony can be bought at too high a price. For example, inefficient conditions may be allowed to continue because no one is willing to blow the whistle. There was a time, some years past, when several of the members of the executive committee of DuPont were unwilling to talk with their peers except at scheduled meetings. The executive committee, then as now, was the principal management arm of the company. Clearly the CEO had his work cut out for him.

There are additional facets of the CEO's job in large organizations that warrant attention. They can be summarized as overload, isolation, and limited time for responding to the corporation's human resources challenges. With respect to overload, as we noted earlier, the CEO is held responsible for all aspects of the corporation's performance, present and prospective. In addition to these heavy responsibilities, he has the onus of being the chief articulator and bearer of the corporation's credo and image both internally and externally. This requires that he spend considerable time visiting subsidiary units and representing the corporation in a variety of ways, which may range from attending social functions to testifying before Congress. In recent years, some large corporations have created the "office of the chairman" so that the load can be shared among two or three senior executives. But while the CEO's burdens can be thus lightened, he is still in the place where the buck stops.

To help them deal with their multiple responsibilities, most CEOs rely on a personal staff. But this solution often brings new problems. Many CEOs with competent staff become more and more isolated, especially from those some distance from the top. Such isolation can create considerable resentment. Thus, during World War II General Marshall rankled many Pentagon brass by ignoring them and relying on a Captain Austin Bonus for most of his human resources information. Bonus was the only staff officer who usually accompanied the Chief of Staff when he appeared before Congressional committees. And few CEOs, even if they decide to bypass their senior associates, know the specialists at the lower levels of their organization who would be best able to help them with a specific problem.

One of the most damaging consequences of the crowded schedules that generally govern the lives and activities of CEOs is that CEOs are unable to act and react on a continuing basis with most of their executives. As a result, they are often not as well informed as they should be or would like to be about the capabilities and potential of managers at or near the top of the company. They are forced to rely on what they are told, together with whatever information is provided by the MIS and the performance appraisal system. Because the oral and written evidence about the ability and potential of a manager is always limited and often flawed, the CEO often lacks a basis for making an independent assessment of the more promising individuals on the managerial ladder. And yet such an assessment could be among his most important contributions to the long-term prospects of the corporation.

This, then, is the outline of our thesis. Scale has resulted in an organizational structure that limits the effective utilization of managerial talent, thereby placing the large corporation at risk. We have identified five basic elements in the large corporation that contribute to the underutilization of its human resources—the cushion, the MIS, the performance appraisal system, competition among divisional units, and the CEO. Each of these dimensions is considered at greater length and in more depth in the later chapters, where we will also discuss ways in which their adverse impacts can be moderated.

PART II

Perspectives

2

Large Organizations

In this chapter, the first of four in which we seek a broader perspective on the impact of organizational scale on the utilization of corporate personnel, we focus on other types of large organizations. Our aim will be to determine to what extent scale alone has major dysfunctional effects on how managerial personnel are utilized. In this connection, we shall consider a variety of large organizations, many much older than the modern corporation and some even younger. Thus we shall look briefly at the Catholic Church, the military, the university, government agencies, foundations, and the academic health center. The distinguished business historian Alfred Chandler has advanced the thesis that "structure follows function," which suggests that the large corporation has developed its organizational form in response to changing opportunities to grow and increase its profits. To what extent is it true that scale affects the ways in which all organizations, nonprofit and profit alike, use their human resources?

The Catholic Church

Many writers on organization have termed the Catholic Church the most venerable large institution in the West, as it has achieved and maintained a position of leadership and power for over a millenium and a half. A key organizational characteristic of the Church is that despite its size it has avoided excessive layering. Between the parish priest and the pope, there are only two basic levels, namely, the bishop and the archbishop or cardinal. Another important characteristic is that the parish priest is entrusted with a great deal of authority and responsibility. He is expected to perform a wide array of functions involving matters of faith and ceremonial practice, as well as management duties such as raising and disbursing the considerable sums of money required to operate the parish services.

Persons, property, and power are always intermingled in organizational performance, growth, and survival, and that has surely been the case in the long history of the Catholic Church. Although the property the Church has owned and the power it has wielded have varied from one time and place to another, never has either of these elements been absent. They were and are essential to the Church's continued growth and survival.

Another factor that has contributed to the long-term strength of the Church is its unique human resources policies. The basic building blocks have included an elaborate educational structure, from parish schools to papal universities, which has assured a stream of dedicated leaders as well as a mass of followers; the establishment and nurturing of a large number of orders and congregations, whose members pursue specialized missions, which reinforce the purposes and goals of the Church; and the vows of celibacy taken by priests and nuns, which have tied them more closely to the Church's central mission.

In a world characterized by conflict—religious, political, economic, ideological, racial, and ethnic—and by changes that are often in direct conflict with Church doctrine and dogma, the Church continues to survive. It has coped with repeated threats and challenges from the outside and it has protected and propagated its traditions, teachings, and beliefs, which have been and remain the foundations of its strength.

In the context of this inquiry, which is focused on the

interactions among scale, organization, and managerial performance, we must conclude that over the centuries the Church leadership has developed an extraordinary skill in coping with the new without surrendering the essentials of the old. Thus John XXIII made a number of belated adjustments to align the Church more closely with the post–World War II environment, and Paul VI and John Paul II have had to seek a new balance to insure that the inherited structure could survive Pope John's multiple reforms. Clearly scale and complexity have not prevented the Catholic Church from adjusting successfully to challenges from without and within.

As the twentieth century draws to a close, the Church faces many serious challenges, especially in the affluent West and from within its own ranks. Recruitment to the clergy and the orders has become more difficult; a large number of priests and nuns have requested and received permission to be released from their vows; and a sizable and vocal minority is pressing for the elimination of the vows of celibacy. Many of the laity are requesting a larger role in the decision making of the Church, and a growing number have decided to rely on their consciences rather than on their priests for decisions on a range of critical matters, including birth control and divorce. The drop in recruitment is in itself a matter of great concern. As was pointed out in an April 14, 1984, article in *The Economist,* the Catholic Church in America "will soon have a serious manpower problem. There are fewer than 12,000 seminarians studying for the priesthood now compared with 48,000 in 1965—and only 60 percent are expected to take their final vows."

We can find some interesting parallels between the Church and the large corporation when we look at the pervasive discontent in the middle ranks of both hierarchies, a discontent leading in each case to demands for more freedom and initiative. Both institutions are currently threatened by potentially costly resignations and recruitment difficulties if they do not accommodate to these demands.

However, only a rash observer would conclude from these

losses and prospective losses that the Church will not be able to surmount this crisis, as it has surmounted earlier ones. It remains the most successful large organization in the history of the world as a result of its ability to attract, indoctrinate, and retain a broad leadership cadre, whose principal duties are, in turn, directed to conditioning the beliefs, lives, and actions of the large numbers of parishioners. But both the Church's organizational structure and its human resources policies are faced with great challenges as we approach the end of the twentieth century.

The Military

The military as it exists in advanced industrial societies provides a different but equally important insight into the critical relations between organizational structure and manpower utilization. Of particular relevance, of course, are times of major mobilization and war, when victory becomes the overriding national objective. We focus here on the experience of the U.S. Army (which included the Air Corps) in World War II, the largest single organized effort in our nation's history.

First, it is worth recalling that between 1940 and 1945 the Army expanded about thirtyfold, from about 270,000 to over 8.2 million. This rapid expansion was facilitated by the fact that many officers in the regular army had gained experience by participating in the New Deal's Civilian Conservation Corps. A few, such as Brehon B. Somervell, had other valuable experience as civilian administrators. Somervell had served in New York City in 1939–1940 as Mayor La Guardia's WPA administrator and had been responsible for the construction of La Guardia Airport, good preparation for a man whose first assignment in Washington was to build the Pentagon. Somervell's outstanding performance in New York City surely helps to explain why he was chosen to head the Services of Supply (later renamed the

Large Organizations

Army Services Forces) after three other senior officers had failed. At its peak, the Army Services Forces employed almost 2 million civilians (twice the size of AT&T when it was the nation's largest employer) and in addition had several hundred thousand military personnel on its rolls. The Army Services Forces was responsible for all supply and service missions, in fact for everything except fighting on the ground and in the air.

In early 1943, Somervell drew up a plan to cut the personnel rolls by about 180,000 civilians within a ninety-day period and to transfer 60,000 soldiers to the Army Ground Forces. Despite the magnitude of the numbers of persons to be separated or reassigned, the plan was carried out with little disruption and some gain in efficiency.

Somervell and his close advisors concluded shortly thereafter that the war presented a unique opportunity to bring about a major structural reform of the army. This reform would involve stripping the seven technical services—Ordnance, Quartermaster, Signal, Transportation, Medical, Engineers, Chemical—of most of their power and restructuring the Army Services Forces into a "functional organization." Months of secret study were spent preparing the detailed plan. It had gained the approval of all of Somervell's superiors except for Secretary of War Henry L. Stimson when one of the technical services heard of it and sought to thwart its implementation through outside help from hostile Congressmen and antiadministration press. At that point, the plan became one more piece on the crowded chessboard involved in the selection of a commander for Overlord (the code name for the forthcoming invasion of Europe) and, in the event that General Marshall were chosen, the selection of a successor for Marshall as Chief of Staff. Roosevelt finally decided that Marshall and Somervell would remain in their posts, and Stimson concluded that it was too risky to restructure the Army Service Forces in the middle of the war, particularly since the existing organization was performing satisfactorily.

Several lessons can be extracted from the foregoing sketch.

First, even a war does not bring to a halt the power struggles among competing military groups. Second, as the Secretary of War decided, regardless of the plan's logic and long-term efficiency, the potential for short-run organizational turmoil was too great. Better to live with the extant organization than to risk precipitating conflicts that might get out of control. Finally, military discipline notwithstanding, when the technical chiefs learned that they might lose their commands, they did not hesitate to breach discipline and seek aid on the outside. Such power struggles, along with balancing the risks versus the gains from organizational reforms, are also characteristic of large corporations.

There is broad agreement among the experts that General George C. Marshall was the chief architect of victory, the one indispensable man. In the prewar years, Marshall had been stationed at Fort Benning, the principal training post for the infantry. While at Benning he filled a small notebook with entries on each of the young officers who came under his scrutiny, and he later used this notebook in making his selections for division, corps, and army commanders.

No matter how good the record keeping, however, evidence from peacetime can prove misleading when the fighting begins. Eisenhower had to remove a senior field commander in North Africa because he had established his command post too far behind the front. Moreover, a combat leader usually has no second chance to prove himself. Men want to be led by a winner. Eisenhower recognized his shortage of aggressive commanders and therefore protected the crusty, outrageous General George Patton, not once but several times, from an irate press and publicity-seeking politicians.

In early 1944 the then Undersecretary of the Army, Robert P. Patterson, distressed by domestic strikes that were interfering with shipments of ammunition to the soldiers at the front, recommended to the Congress on his own, without Pentagon backing, that it pass a National Service Act giving the federal

Large Organizations

government control over the entire civilian labor force. No person would be permitted to change jobs, move to a new location, or make any other job change without prior approval of the government. The bill did not pass because of fears that the government would be unable to use such a broad grant of power effectively. An army that had failed earlier to stay within the numerical ceiling established by the Congress by more than 600,000 was not to be trusted with absolute control over the entire civilian work force.

The U.S. experience in World War II revealed the importance of organization in achieving victory over the enemy. But organization alone was not enough. It was also necessary to identify able men and assign them to key positions of leadership. The army was fortunate that many officers who had contemplated resigning during the prosperous 1920s decided to remain on active duty during the Depression. It was also fortunate that General Pershing was still alive when it became necessary to select a new chief of staff in 1939. But for Pershing it is doubtful that Marshall would have been selected.

The U.S. experience, both on the home front and in the theaters of war, revealed that struggles among organizational units and among the senior leaders who commanded them were not suspended "for the duration." On the contrary, they consumed much of the time and energy of our leaders. Forty years after the event, Eisenhower's handling of Montgomery continues to engage military historians. Many contend that the credit Montgomery claimed for the victories that the Allied forces achieved far exceeded his contribution to those victories. And almost all military analysts agree that Montgomery's behavior on more than one occasion amounted to insubordination that Eisenhower decided to overlook.

The war also underscored the important fact that more is not always better. The Army Services Forces certainly, and probably the Army as a whole, had reached a point in late 1943 where further growth would have been dysfunctional. The costs of

35

managing still larger numbers would probably not have been repaid by their contributions within the compressed time period when the final campaigns were to be launched. One impressive lesson of the war was the willingness of millions of men to tolerate all sorts of organizational inefficiency, stupidity, confusion, and on occasion outright cupidity because they realized that scale was the primary villain and that tolerance of the malfunctioning system was a necessary price for victory.

The problems of scale and their effect on manpower utilization—specifically, large overhead costs, the difficulties of deploying resources when and where needed, and assuming that chosen targets were the right ones—did not evaporate with the cessation of fighting. On the contrary, they were a major challenge to the Department of Defense, established early in the postwar years to unify the armed forces. Some years ago, the then Deputy Secretary of Defense and Secretary of State had to decide which of the two departments would issue a press release about a subject of little moment. When, after a lengthy telephone conversation by the principals, the issue was finally settled, the Deputy Secretary of Defense remarked that the system in Washington really didn't make sense: his long telephone call left him twenty-five minutes for his next appointment with an Air Force general who required his signature on a $5 billion contract for the procurement of new planes.

There are other difficulties involved in effectively managing large government departments. This particular Deputy Secretary of Defense had to carry a disproportionate share of responsibility. The reason for this was that the Secretary of Defense, despite having achieved a top position in corporate life, was only marginally effective in Washington, where he often had to operate in the open, unprotected by staff. For the record, it should be observed that the reverse is also true. For every Lucius Clay, who performed out of uniform almost as well as in uniform, there have been many senior officers who chalked up only mediocre records as corporate leaders.

Large Organizations

In the waning years of the Truman administration and the early years of Eisenhower's, four individuals served as Assistant Secretary of the Army for Manpower and Reserve Affairs. Their average term in office was less than two years, much of it spent visiting foreign bases. There was no way, even for a well-prepared, able, and hard-working official, to make a lasting impact on a complex department in so brief a term. Any slim prospect for doing so was effectively killed by the fact that the assistant secretary had to be constantly involved in routine military matters of little or no consequence. This involvement left him little time or energy to develop an independent position on critical policy issues.

The Department of Defense has had many able secretaries, who have been, on average, more talented than other cabinet officers. Yet throughout its existence the department has not been subject to effective civilian control. Each of the three services guards its prerogatives and independence; each is in continuing and intense competition with the other two over missions and resources; and each controls the careers of its officers who are assigned to the Office of the Secretary of Defense. The top civilian officials in the department are primarily dependent on their military staffs, whose spokesmen and advocates they inevitably become.

In 1970, the Defense Science Board appointed a committee to review and recommend changes in the management of military manpower. At that time military manpower consumed almost half of the department's annual budget. After working conscientiously for the better part of a year, the committee issued its report. But even if those at the top were agreeable, there was no way to bring about significant changes given the lack of interest, lack of cooperation, and often outright opposition of one or more of the services. Those who favored the reforms were too weak to overcome the opposition of the Services, which balked at making any significant change in their spheres of control over personnel. Eighteen months later, when a newly appointed Secretary of Defense asked to see a copy of the committee's report, *Manpower Management in Large Organizations,* the Office of the Assistant Secretary of Defense for Manpower was thrown into a flap: it could not retrieve a single copy.

The Department of Defense is proof positive that organizations can reach a scale and complexity where effective leadership and management is no longer possible. Such elephantine organizations seem to be essentially self-propelled, with successive cohorts of professionals providing the necessary energy to keep them going. Those at the top come and go, leaving little trace. A reasonable presumption is that the other superpower confronts much the same situation. There is some comfort in this observation. It was the Pentagon's conventional wisdom during World War II that our eventual victory depended on our being a little more efficient than our enemies. Competition in the public sector, as in the private, assumes that victory goes to the least inefficient.

Indeed, there are some interesting parallels to the problems and issues recounted above that our largest corporations confront in kind if not in degree. For example, just as a good record in peacetime is no guarantee that a general will perform well under fire, so business leaders who do well in one environment often are ineffective in another. A skilled cost-cutter may be ill-suited to head a corporation during a period of expansion. Nevertheless, knowledge of subordinates' past performance is important, in the corporation as in the military. General Marshall's keeping a notebook with critical assessments of the performance and potential of promising officers is a practice that few senior corporate executives emulate.

To give another parallel, just as the Secretary of War refused to authorize a promising plan for reorganizing the Army Services Forces because of the risks and costs involved, so many a CEO has pulled back from making desirable, even necessary, changes in his organization because he believed that the costs would turn out to be excessive.

Large Organizations

The University

The University is both an old and new type of large organization. The major European centers of learning date from the twelfth and thirteenth centuries. The spectacular growth of American universities, however, took place during the present century, particularly since the end of World War II. The precipitating factors were the explosion of government funding for research and development and the opening of universities to all qualified students. Today, institutions such as Harvard, Yale, and Columbia, as well as the principal state-supported universities in the Midwest and far West, have students and faculty numbering in the tens of thousands, total revenue flows in the multi-hundreds of millions, and endowments that occasionally exceed one billion. Let us look more closely at Columbia, one of these universities.

In the late 1920s Columbia was the lengthened shadow of Nicholas Murray Butler, its president. In the quarter century that he had been at the helm, Columbia had been transformed from a small, parochial institution into one of the most distinguished academic centers in the world. Butler had a vision; he had obtained the necessary resources; and he had appointed the key deans and directors, who helped him transform the institution.

Then came the Great Depression, and the process of development was halted and then reversed. Resources became increasingly constrained, and appointments to the faculty were frozen. But in Columbia's case the problems brought on by the Depression were compounded by an internal factor. The man at the helm, who had already passed his sixty-seventh birthday when the stock market collapsed, gradually lost his bearings, his health, and his spirit. Nevertheless, he stayed on as president until 1945. The board of trustees, which he had so long dominated, lacked the judgment and the courage to request his resignation.

The story of the succession follows: Frank Fackenthal was acting president for a few years; he was followed by Dwight David Eisenhower, who spent two years of his five-year term as president at SHAPE (Supreme Headquarters Allied Powers Europe); Grayson Kirk became the incumbent in 1952 and remained until the student crisis of 1968; another short interregnum under Andrew Cordier finally culminated in the appointment of William McGill in 1970. For forty years (1930–1970) Columbia had been without strong leadership, and this lack had seriously weakened the institution. What is remarkable is that because of its strong departmental structure, selected units were able to remain at the forefront while the institution lost momentum.

There are different ways to read this encapsulated history of one major university. Emphasis can be placed on the inertial power of a large institution to keep itself afloat despite weakness at the top. A more pessimistic reading would stress that while weakness at the top can be ignored for a time, it eventually takes a toll. A third reading is that after a period of floundering, an institution that has succeeded in remaining afloat may, under strong leadership, make a comeback. That is the hope and promise of Columbia under Michael I. Sovern in the mid-1980s.

World War II and its aftermath led to explosive growth in the scale, scope, and financing of U.S. universities. In the prewar decades, when no more than about one in every twenty young persons graduated from college, well-endowed nonprofit institutions were able to meet a significant proportion of their total operating expenses from earnings on their endowments and other philanthropic income. In the postwar years, everything exploded—the number of students, faculty, administrators, supporting staff, salaries, federally sponsored research, student loans—at the same time that earnings from endowments were being eroded by an accelerating inflation, which also put heavy pressure on operating costs. Colleges and universities were reluctant to make large annual increases in their tuition, until they finally saw no alternative. From that point on, they realized that

Large Organizations

for better or worse they were in the money economy to stay.

Once a university could no longer look to eleemosynary sources for balancing its budget, the income-raising potential of the various schools and departments became a matter of critical importance. And if the overall financial position of the institution was straitened, money considerations came to dominate the environment. In most universities, the income-generating units tend to be of two sorts: prestigious departments (that is, those with well-known faculty) and professional schools, particularly in medicine, law, and business. Such units did not relish having their surplus revenues drained off to pay for salaries of professors in other departments, no matter how great their distinction or their need. But universities, like nonprofit hospitals, have always engaged in "cross-subsidization." It is not possible for a large university to exist and flourish unless a considerable number of departments are assisted by dollar transfers from major divisions that make a "profit" or incur only small losses. A large corporation also "cross-subsidizes" a new unit, but after a time the unit must earn profits or it will be liquidated. Not so in a university; some departments require ongoing subsidization.

Another striking organizational characteristic of the major universities is the distinction between the formal hierarchy and the effective distribution of power. Although the president appoints the deans and the deans appoint department chairmen, the members of the teaching faculty—from the most distinguished professor to the most recently appointed lecturer—rule supreme in their classrooms. Early in General Eisenhower's brief sojourn on Morningside Heights he was told at a faculty meeting, "Sir, you don't understand; we are the university!" Since a tenured professor can be removed only for "cause" (and this act is subject to external review, which may lead to the university being blacklisted if procedures are found wanting), one is inclined to agree with General Eisenhower's interlocutor.

One final observation about how large universities have responded to changes affecting their scale, scope, and complexity.

41

They have built up large administrative structures in order to cope more effectively with new responsibilities in areas ranging from much-expanded fund raising efforts to compliance with the federal government's rules and regulations governing R&D grants and contracts. Some disgruntled professors who find their salaries lagging behind inflation ascribe their worsening position to the growth of university overhead. But the same diffusion of power that enables the faculty to go its way also enables the administration to move in the nonacademic areas without serious check. The inept and intimidated board of trustees that permitted Dr. Butler to remain in office long after he should have retired has its counterpart in the world of large corporations. Boards of directors have repeatedly failed to insist on the resignation of a CEO who has passed his peak but refuses to leave.

As large corporations recruit and employ larger numbers of professionals, particularly research scientists with a national or international reputation, they must face a problem that the university confronted years ago. They cannot treat persons of renown as hired hands; they cannot expect them meekly to follow orders that are passed down from the top. But neither can these talented individuals have free access to the corporation's research funds. The solutions must still be developed for this and related problems of effectively integrating high-powered professionals into the large corporation.

The Government Agency

The prototypical contrast to the large business enterprise is not the Church, the military, or the university—each of which predates the large corporation by centuries—but rather, the large government agency. Scholars from Max Weber to Anthony Downs have discussed, both theoretically and empirically, how

Large Organizations

government bureaucracies act and react. But although generalizations across countries are possible, ultimately governmental structures are embedded in a nation's history, traditions, and values. Since we cannot deal with them as a genotype even though they share certain characteristics, we will focus on U.S. federal government agencies.

A good place to begin is with the facts on turnover. The head of the federal government, the president, is elected for a four-year term, and with each new incumbent there is a turnover of about two thousand senior political appointees, responsible for managing departments and agencies whose combined annual expenditures will approach the $1 trillion level in 1985.

Preparations for a presidential election usually get underway at least a year in advance, and a new administration usually needs the larger part of a year to settle in. This means that effective executive oversight of major federal departments and agencies extends over no more than half of each four-year span, except when a president is reelected—and sometimes not even then, as Nixon's radical shake-up of the executive branch at the outset of his second administration demonstrated.

It has often been stated that no individual elected to the presidency is prepared for the job. For example, early in President Kennedy's administration, the newspapers carried an item that he had instructed the members of his cabinet to forward to him, twice weekly, a summary of all policy actions. Not long after this, a second item reported that the president had canceled his earlier directive. He had recognized that he did not have the time to read the reports and that he was in no position to undertake follow-up actions.

But Kennedy, like other presidents, learned quickly. Shortly after this episode, upon reviewing a position paper that had been prepared for him, he commented that he found it persuasive but added that "he didn't know whether the government of the United States was in agreement with it." As Kennedy had discovered, the power of the White House to persuade the bureaucracy is limited if the senior officials are opposed to taking action.

The president and his political appointees account for only two-thirds of the managerial cadre. The remaining third consists of the members of the permanent civil service, unflatteringly dubbed "bureaucrats." These individuals have made a decision to spend some or all of their working lives in a government agency, carrying out the functions assigned to it by law and presidential directive.

The government bureaucrat is commonly caricatured as an individual who contributes little that is useful to the society or the economy; who shuffles papers for a few hours each day; who comes and goes by the clock and spends much of his time away from his desk in the coffee shop or at the water cooler; and who is most faithful about collecting his check.

More sophisticated critics call attention to a different array of shortcomings: bureaucrats do not have to meet a market test of earning a profit; they often enter into cozy long-term relations with the chairmen of the congressional committees that authorize their budgets; and many are adept in protecting their turf and have learned how to wait out their revolving-door political bosses. There are clearly "federal" responsibilities embedded in the Constitution and in later legislative enactments, and they surely involve more than paper shuffling. After all, two out of every three civilian federal employees are engaged in delivering the mail, helping veterans, or supporting the Armed Services.

On behalf of the commission he headed, J. Peter Grace submitted, at the end of 1983, a report to President Reagan that listed a set of reforms in the federal government—reforms that could result in savings of over $400 billion within a three-year period. This is not the first, nor will it be the last, time that a prestigious committee of business leaders has drawn up such a list. For example, outside consultants are usually called in when corporations confront difficult and sometimes intractable problems that the chief executive is unwilling to tackle or cannot easily resolve on his own.

The corporate world itself makes heavy use of outside consultants. The last decades have seen a striking growth in management consulting firms, which earn most of their income from corporate clients. Often, consultants are a way to overcome barriers to change. In such cases, the chief executive's hope is that, with a strong report in hand and the management softened by repeated meetings with the consulting staff, he will be better positioned to gain his subordinates' support for the changes he favors.

In the federal arena, however, the barriers to change are even greater. The overworked Executive Office of the President must first determine which of a large number of recommendations submitted by prestigious outside groups make sense. It must then seek to persuade the major agencies to support—or at least not oppose—the proposed changes. But most of the critical improvements require congressional action, and here is where most reforms founder. The president and the Congress find it difficult, frequently impossible, to agree, and as time passes, the momentum behind the reform dissipates.

Let us assume, as seems reasonable, that individuals who enter and remain in federal employment are little different from individuals employed in the private sector. Let us assume that they seek useful work and that they look forward to reasonable remuneration and other rewards for their efforts. Given these assumptions, we cannot agree with those who see federal agencies as inherently nonproductive, resource-wasting, and self-aggrandizing organizations. Their view is a misrepresentation, but one that has deep roots.

To begin with, the functions of government differ from the functions of business. Politicans and corporate executives pursue different ends through different means. Just as large corporations are constrained by government, government itself is constrained by, and must rely on, the private sector. Consider the following example. The Department of Defense buys almost all of its weapons systems from large corporations. As new weapons come on stream, overruns in the hundreds of millions of dollars are not unusual, and after review most of the additional costs are usually approved. There is no effective market to provide buyers and sellers with proper guidance.

And it is not just the private sector on which the government must rely. Over the last third of a century the National Institutes of Health have expanded their annual support for biomedical research from $65 million to over $4 billion. By far the largest proportion of these large annual appropriations go to colleges and universities. Awards are based on the recommendations of peer review groups, subject to approval by advisory councils.

Over the period 1962–1982, the federal government appropriated about $100 billion for employment and training under MDTA and CETA legislation. By the end of the 1960s, when the federal government realized that it could not effectively manage the 10,000 or more individual training programs, it delegated responsibility to about 450 prime sponsors, primarily state and large city governments.

We can see, then, that federal agencies are engaged in carrying out congressional mandates and that the effectiveness with which they do so depends primarily on the capability (and the integrity) of other sectors of the society—large corporations, universities, lower levels of government, nonprofit hospitals (Medicare). If we take this into account, we can understand some of the differences between business and government. But despite their differences, large agencies and large business enterprises share a number of characteristics related to scale. The difficulties of implementing changes are, as we saw, one such characteristic.

The Large Foundation

The large foundation, with an independent board of trustees, is another relatively new large organization, in existence for less

Large Organizations

than a century. The Ford Foundation is the largest, with over $3.4 billion of assets and annual grants of about $160 million. Benefactors specify purposes and goals, but over the years, the original specifications carry less weight as the public board of trustees comes increasingly to control policy and outlays. Some years ago, Henry Ford II became sufficiently disenchanted with the directions the Ford Foundation was taking that, after losing the battle in the boardroom, he resigned and severed all connections with the foundation. Large philanthropic foundations make annual grants, mostly in the $10–50 million range, for public programs running the gamut from support for artists to medical research and the advancement of civil rights.

The management structures of large foundations differ in a number of dimensions: the extent to which the trustees are active, the extent to which the president is expected to provide direction, the amount of discretion allowed senior program officers, and the degree of reliance placed on outside consultants. But the differences are not as great as the similarities.

Large foundations believe that they have a benign influence on public and private programs, practice, and policy. They say to themselves, and to each other, that their principal charge is to innovate and test new approaches to solving societal problems. Since they want their programs to make a difference—preferably a large difference in a small number of years, usually less than five—they find it difficult to discover sufficiently exciting projects and even more difficult to design such projects.

Because of the shortage of attractive projects and the large number of requests for funding, far beyond their resources, individual foundations are increasingly joining with others to provide support. This not only stretches their dollars, but allows the president and staff to reassure the trustees that other foundations have found the proposals to have merit.

The last few decades have also seen the growth of foundations funded by large corporations; these foundations make significant grants to communities in which the corporation has a sizable presence in addition to underwriting important cultural and educational efforts. Another change has been the moves on the part of most public foundations to diversify their trustees. For example, several of the largest foundations have deliberately sought to add leaders from minority groups.

As is often the case where there is no market test—and to some extent even when such a test exists—foundations are hard pressed to assess the effectiveness of the programs they fund. Many of the larger foundations obtain both inside and outside evaluations of their important programs. The Robert Wood Johnson Foundation, in the medical field, routinely builds outside evaluations into its grant making. Despite such efforts, assessing outcomes in terms of leverage, time, impact, and lasting results is difficult. Whereas government outlays in social welfare— health, education, welfare, and social services—in 1982 totaled over one half a trillion dollars, the combined expenditures of all foundations for these same purposes came to just over $1 billion. The discrepancy between the two sums, especially when placed in the context of our earlier observation that foundations are reluctant to fund a particular effort for more than a few years, suggests how difficult it is for them to contribute to a significant change in social attitudes and behavior. For every Myrdal study on *An American Dilemma* or the Green Revolution there are hundreds and thousands of foundation projects that have little lasting impact.

In this difficult environment, the heads of the principal foundations have assumed a product-design, marketing role. They take the ideas of their staffs or outside proposals and attempt to shape them to the preferences and predilections of their trustees. The task is sufficiently complex, and those who perform well are sufficiently few, that the role of a foundation executive is now recognized as a specialized profession. Although smaller in scale, less complex in structure, and working with a much smaller staff, usually in the tens or scores, foundations

Large Organizations

resemble other large organizations in their ability to respond to changing opportunities and in the bureaucratic tendencies that come to dominate their decision making.

The Academic Health Center

The last type of large organization that we will briefly inspect, the academic health center, is both the youngest and from an organizational and management point of view the most complex. The academic health center dates from the post–World War II era, when the federal government decided to become a major underwriter of biomedical research and to direct most of its funds to medical schools and universities. In 1983, federal allocations for biomedical research totaled $5.5 billion, and funding from all sources totaled over $9 billion. About 50 percent of this total went to academic medicine.

An academic health center is defined as an organizational arrangement, usually under the auspices of a university, consisting of a medical school and its major teaching hospital(s) and at least one other health professional school (dental, nursing, public health, pharmacy, veterinary medicine, and others). All medical schools require one or more teaching hospital affiliates; thus the key elements of an academic health center are the university, the medical school, and the teaching hospital.

The arrangements among these principals vary greatly. At one extreme, represented by Harvard, principal teaching affiliates are independent institutions except for the fact that key staff have joint appointments. At the other extreme, represented by New York University and the University of Chicago, the university is the owner-operator of the major teaching hospital. The total dollar flow passing through a major academic health center during the course of a year for teaching, research, and patient care can be in excess of $300 million. The actual amount is largely determined by the size of the teaching hospital and the amount of research funds that the center is able to attract.

Unless the university owns and operates both the medical school and the hospital, the organizational and management structures tend to be complex. This complexity has adverse effects on the efficient use of resources, both dollars and personnel. While universities affiliated with medical schools tend to have but a single board of trustees, which has responsibility for all of the academic departments and schools, the medical school often has its own board, which oversees its operations and helps with fund raising. In turn, most major teaching hospitals are independent entities, with their own boards responsible for policy and direction. In order to bring about some degree of conjoint action at the board level, the cooperating institutions—or at least, the two most directly involved, the medical school and the teaching hospital—may establish a new board or designate some members to a joint board. Such a joint board has some degree of oversight, although the legal power for decision making is likely to be retained by the principals—the university and, in cases where it is independent, the hospital.

These complexities that arise with boards of trustees have their counterpart in day-to-day management. In some cases, the dean of the medical school must negotiate on all issues with his counterpart, the director of the hospital. In other cases, a director is appointed to manage the medical center, and the dean and hospital director both report to him. In such instances the medical center director usually reports to the two independent boards.

The complexities continue. The heads of the major clinical departments in the medical school are also the chiefs of services in the hospital. In each environment, there is a different reporting line to a different management structure. Although the cash flow has tended to make the hospital the dominant partner, the professional base and prestige of the chiefs of services are centered in the medical school.

Even this formulation oversimplifies the situation. The clinical chiefs, as well as the heads of the basic science departments in the medical school, enjoy considerable independence through their external research funding. The dean of the medical school is often more indebted to them than they are to him. Their direct access to external funding makes them barons, each with his fiefdom, and they brook little direction and no dictation from the school's administration.

This convoluted management structure and the multiple sources of funding have led to major changes in the operation of the academic medical center during recent decades. Illustrative of these changes has been the explosion in the ratio of faculty members to medical students, which is now approaching 1:1. For example, in a major department at a major teaching hospital (such as the Department of Medicine at Johns Hopkins), the number of salaried members has increased over the last decades from about twenty to over two hundred.

The multiple sources of funding for education, research, and patient care have also led to more and larger residency and fellowship programs, all of which carry stipends. Since residents and fellows are heavily involved in both overseeing patient care and providing apprenticeship training for advanced medical students and first-year house staff, their superiors have more time to pursue their own interests—research, practice, or both.

The one unequivocal conclusion we can draw from this sketch of trends in large academic health centers is that freely flowing money combined with a convoluted management structure led inevitably to empire building, excessive staffing, and less than optimal personnel utilization. Total annual outlays for hospital care, a significant part of which is provided by the teaching hospitals, skyrocketed between 1950 and 1984—from around $3.5 billion to over $150 billion!

The Effects of Scale

We now turn to the question of whether, and to what extent, the problems of these large nonbusiness organizations—the Church, the military, universities, government agencies, foundations, and academic health centers—parallel those of the large corporation. What influences does scale, separate from function, have on the effectiveness with which key human resources, professional and managerial, are deployed? To answer this question we will return to our discussion, introduced in chapter 1, of the five areas in which the large corporation experiences difficulties because of scale.

We found that financial reserves (the cushion) often enable corporate management to avoid making hard decisions when problems first appear. As was especially clear from the discussion of academic health centers, much the same situation exists among all or most of the not-for-profit organizations. They, too, use their budgetary elasticity to postpone making difficult decisions.

The measurement of performance, our second area, is even more complex in some of these other large institutions than it is in the large corporation. It often takes a war, for example, to reveal weaknesses in the military. And it would be difficult to reach a judgment about how well the Church is carrying out its mission. As with the corporation, the difficulty of measuring performance enables these institutions to continue for long periods in their accustomed ways before finally facing up to new realities.

Personnel evaluations and practices in the various institutions we have looked at are problematic in many of the same ways that they are in the large corporation. Again, it is difficult to sort out performance from preference, and many who advance owe their progress more to their skill in playing the game than to their superior accomplishments.

Large Organizations

At least in some cases, the heads of large not-for-profit organizations may have less difficulty reducing or reapportioning the power and authority of subsidiary units. President Franklin D. Roosevelt had such a low opinion of many of the cabinet departments, particularly State and Treasury, that he established new structures to develop and implement his policies. The recent actions of Pope John Paul II to reduce the autonomy of the Jesuits is another striking example of intervention from the top. On the other hand, no president or secretary of defense, not even Robert McNamara, has ever undertaken and carried through the task of radically reducing the freedom of the individual armed services in favor of a coordinated defense policy.

In the selection of the top executive, corporate and noncorporate large organizations once again disclose more similarities than differences. In both cases, the top executive is often chosen from within. For centuries the Pope has been chosen from among the members of the College of Cardinals. And those who run for the presidency of the United States must have been in the public view for a period of years. It is true that neither Carter nor Reagan was in the forefront of his party before entering the White House. But this is beside the point. Each had served as governor of a state, Reagan for two terms. Each had established a public record that the electorate was in a position to assess. True, the electorate may err in assessing the record and political mettle of those who compete for the nation's highest office. But it is a risk that cannot be avoided. To vote for an unknown, by contrast, is a risk that the electorate refuses to take. It is almost half a century since a rank outsider, Wendell Willkie, was nominated by the Republican Party.

We have identified a number of similarities between the large corporation and other large organizations that are the direct consequences of their accommodations to the imperatives of scale. Each depends for its leadership cadre on college and university graduates. Each seeks to attract and retain the best personnel by relying on a system of internal promotion. In the course of institutionalizing its policies and operations, each is forced to release considerable authority and responsibility to its middle managers.

Each relies on a formal performance rating system to assure that the organization has an objective record of what junior and middle managers have accomplished and of their special strengths and weaknesses. Each places considerable weight on how effectively their managers have demonstrated an ability to get along with their superiors and their peers, since in every large organization this is considered to be a prerequisite for the successful leader. Each has established formal criteria for succession, so that when members of the leadership cadre must step down, the organization will continue to function effectively.

But the search for parallels based on scale should not obscure important differences. The requirement of celibacy is unique to the Catholic Church. The military has tended to enforce a relatively low age of retirement for most officers. The university, as we saw, has an unusual balance of power between the individual professor and the administration. The middle-level and senior civil servant operates in an environment in which he or she can usually be dismissed only on grounds of gross malperformance, charges that must be sustained on review. Government officials must accommodate to frequent changes in the political appointees who have broad policy oversight over their agencies and their work; and if a conflict arises they may be reassigned to positions that will make little or no use of their skills and experience.

Even after allowance has been made for the significant differences among large organizations that stem from differences in their goals, purposes, and methods of operation, the element of scale looms large. Each of the organizations we have discussed must accommodate to the exigencies of scale. Each must keep adjusting its organizational structure and decision-making mechanisms to cope with the problems engendered by scale if it is to elicit the effective participation of all members of its work force.

Large Organizations

A large organization that does not make effective use of its human resources will inevitably suffer an erosion of its position. It will no longer be able to enhance its values and goals, which alone justify its continued existence. Here the large corporation perhaps has an advantage: by virtue of operating in the marketplace it is under more pressure than the other organizations to use effectively all of its resources, including its human resources.

3

Economists and the Corporation

Since economics has been concerned with elucidating the forces that determine the allocation of resources in the marketplace, it is only proper to ask what the leading economists have to offer by way of insight and understanding into the role and performance of the large corporation.

The simple fact is that economists have been so intent on studying what transpires in the marketplace that they have devoted little attention to the large corporation—how it is organized, how it makes decisions, how it uses its managerial personnel. We believe that despite this relative neglect, we must still pay attention to what economists have said about the corporation to see how this relates to our basic concern with the impact of scale on managerial behavior.

Early Formulations

When Adam Smith first described the operations of the competitive model in his *Wealth of Nations* (1776), he focused attention on the haggling between producers and consumers in the marketplace. Smith postulated that each producer would seek to obtain the highest price he could for his wares and each consumer would seek to buy as cheaply as possible. This mutual pursuit of self-interest would assure the production of the largest possible output at the lowest possible price. Since most enterprises were run by a capitalist owner-manager, Smith paid little attention to the internal mechanism of the business—its structure, operations, and decision making.

Adam Smith's entrepreneur, then, was a small businessman. His activities were bounded by the capital that he had available to invest and reinvest. The scale of his operations was limited by the number of persons he could oversee and the number of purchases and sales that he could make. Smith realized that his capitalist-owner-manager could hire one or more foremen or supervisors to oversee the work force and to keep his books. But his critical assumption was that only the owner-manager would make key business decisions—what to buy and sell, when to buy and sell, how much to buy and sell, whom to hire, and how much and when to invest. It was the owner who placed his capital at risk, and he alone could assure its safety and growth.

In Smith's schema, the behavior of all businessmen was determined by the impersonal actions of the market. Changes in prices would assure that demand and supply were kept in reasonable balance. The self-regulating market kept the system in an equilibrium which would determine where more resources were needed and where they were in excess and should be withdrawn. The challenge facing every businessman was to produce and sell at a cost below that of his competitors. In that way he could insure that he would have customers and would make a profit. In Smith's day no businessman was in a position to affect the market through his own actions. All he could hope to do was to adjust to it better than his competitors.

The first serious critique of the efficacy of the market as a mechanism for assuring optimal use of scarce resources came from Karl Marx and his followers. Marx challenged the classical economists by asserting that cumulative rather than equilibrating forces tend to dominate the market. The forces of technology, monopoly, and unemployment were all eroding capitalism's base. Marx's criticism of the classical economists and contemporary capitalism won many converts, especially in Europe, which periodically suffered economic reversals. But the long-term trends in employment and real income were favorable, and modern industrialism became entrenched.

The Business Organization

It was not until the end of the nineteenth century, when Alfred Marshall undertook the formidable task of reconciling classical economics with the capitalism of his day, that a more sophisticated view of business organization emerged. In his *Principles of Economics* (1890) Marshall added a fourth factor of production. That is, to land, labor, and capital, he added organization (or management). He then used this insight to modify the inherited doctrine. The law of diminishing returns— the bedrock of classical economics—held that after a certain point the addition of a factor of production to a parcel of land would lead to a lower relative output. Marshall argued that this might not apply to the manufacturing sector, where increasing returns from additional inputs might be achievable over long periods of time.

Marshall wrote during a period of great changes in corporate structure. The joint-stock company was increasingly dominating the business environment and was providing more scope in the selection and succession of business leaders. But Marshall recognized that such changes in corporate structure would not in themselves resolve the challenge of entrepreneurship. Marshall noted that the successful businessman was likely to slacken his efforts with time and, in any case, he was mortal. The odds were against his sons having his particular combination of energy and ability.

Marshall acknowledged that a publicly owned stock company could grow faster and make its position more secure. But he added a prescient observation: "But it is likely to have lost so much of its elasticity and progressive force, that the advantages are no longer exclusively on its side in its competition with younger and smaller rivals."

The breadth of Marshall's insight into the increasingly important role of business leadership is apparent from his observations about the weakness of Great Britain relative to Germany and the United States. In Britain, Marshall pointed out, the dominant value structure tended to channel the ablest individuals into government service. Imperial Germany, meanwhile, was taking giant steps to establish close linkages among science, technology, and industry. And in the United States, enormous national resources and a continental market created such inviting opportunities that men with energy and vision were inevitably drawn to the world of business. No other sector could match its allure.

Marshall's favorable reading of the American scene was not shared by Thorstein Veblen, one of America's most incisive social critics. The iconoclastic Veblen was disturbed by the way in which the United States was evolving at the turn of the century, the era of the robber barons. He called attention to the widening discrepancy between the theory of business enterprise—a theory of small businessmen competing with one another to increase efficiency and decrease cost, which neoclassical economists used as their point of departure—and the mounting evidence that the quasi-monopolistic large corporation dominated ever larger sectors of the economy, especially in manufacturing, finance, and transportation.

As Veblen observed, these large corporations were under little pressure from the market to be efficient and to operate at or close to full capacity. They were able to optimize their profits by restricting their output and raising their prices, actions at variance with the postulates of competitive theory. In addition, able promoters such as J. P. Morgan focused their considerable ability and energy on the manipulation of "pecuniary values" (i.e., stock prices), rather than on increasing the efficiency of production through improved processes and products.

Veblen's last work, *Absentee Ownership* (1920), is a forceful statement of his critical views. Large firms and large trade unions had freed themselves from the dictates of market forces and were able to pursue a strategy aimed at constricting output and raising prices (or wages), which had adverse effects on the rest of society.

Frank H. Knight's *Risk, Uncertainty and Profit* was published the following year, in 1921. For the most part, it reaffirmed and refined the doctrines of mainline economics, finding little merit in Veblen's criticisms. Knight's most significant contribution was to differentiate the concept of "uncertainty," the distinctive element in his analytic system, from "risk" against which one could insure. The principal task of the entrepreneur, Knight argued, was to deal with uncertainty.

Of greatest relevance to us is Knight's contention that the emergence and growth of large business organizations reflect the gains from both specialization based on scale and the reduction of uncertainty. The ability to cope with uncertainty is the essence of the entrepreneurial function; it is a scarce talent, and large organizations provide one important way to economize its use.

The heads of large corporations are able to develop an implicit contract with the many executive trainees they hire. For a job now and career opportunities later, hired managers are willing to work under direction and control. Knight observes that the key function of the entrepreneur is not to do the directing himself but to select subordinates to help him carry out the critical tasks of control and coordination. According to Knight, these subordinates are called managers but are in reality employees working for wages.

Knight assumed that the classical principle of diminishing

Economists and the Corporation

returns operates in the entrepreneurial realm: "The greater the magnitude of operations which any single individual attempts to direct, the less effective he will be—beyond a certain point" (p. 282). Thus, the principle operated specifically with respect to management: "It is a common and perhaps justifiable opinion that most of the other factors tend toward greater economy with increasing size of the establishment, and that the chief limitation on size is the capacity of the leadership" (p. 283).

Toward the end of the nineteenth century, the American public became concerned about the oppressive powers of the large corporation when the railroads and various trusts in oil, sugar, steel, shoe machinery, and tobacco were using their economic and political muscle to ruin competitors, rig prices, and reap monopoly profits. The Sherman Anti-Trust Act (1890) was enacted in response to these fears. The anti–big business orientation continued with reduced intensity until the passage of the Clayton Act in 1914. Then World War I and the subsequent prosperity of the New Era (1922–1929) dissipated most of earlier concerns and fears about the antisocial behavior of large corporations.

Public distrust of big business reappeared during the Great Depression (1929–1933). In 1932 Adolph Berle, a professor of law at Columbia University, and his research associate, Gardiner Means, published *The Modern Corporation and Private Property*. Here they provided for the first time detailed information, much of it statistical, about the split that had taken place between ownership (the stockholders) and management (the salaried executives responsible for running large corporations). Many executives had only a minute ownership stake in the organizations they managed. At the same time, stock ownership was frequently broadly dispersed among many small holders, who were in no position to influence the chief executive officer, who often selected and dominated his board of directors. The authors made much of the discrepancy between the assumptions of classical economists about the profit-maximizing tendencies of the entrepreneur and their findings that managers had great scope to further their own rather than their stockholders' interests.

Just prior to the publication of their book, Berle and Means talked to the graduate seminar in Economic Theory at Columbia University. They immodestly compared their forthcoming book with Adam Smith's *Wealth of Nations,* startling the seminar. Smith, in his magnum opus, had in fact addressed at length the problems arising out of a split between ownership and management, using the large trading companies as his examples. In Smith's view a division between ownership and control was a certain precursor to inefficiency and waste and could even result in gross corruption and war. He emphasized that as long as the owners received a regular return on their capital, they were only too willing to let the directors run the company, which, he noted, did not necessarily result in optimal returns.

Further, Smith pointed to the inability of directors to control their agents many thousands of miles from the home office. By law and regulation these agents were prohibited from trading on their own account, but this injunction was honored largely in the breach. Moreover, in their avidity for short-term gains, these agents often oppressed the native population, caring little for their welfare or for that of the country in which they traded. On occasion, the agents' policies were so shortsighted that they forced their sovereign into war.

In Smith's view, the only reason that these large trading companies were able to survive was that in return for favors, including large loans, Parliament had given them exclusive grants. By virtue of having no competition, they were able to earn high enough profits to more than compensate for their inefficiencies. Smith's remedy was simple: Parliament should open the trade to all competitors.

Insightful though these comments were, they had never attracted much attention. Most economists simply read them as observations on a bygone age. But the staggering economic losses of the Great Depression brought a renewed concern with the

Economists and the Corporation

behavior of the large corporation, particularly the big banks and holding companies. Congressional investigations in the early 1930s led to extended reform legislation, passed shortly after Roosevelt took office. The new laws and regulations were aimed at restricting the opportunities of insiders to take advantage of special information by speculating in the company's stock, forcing the disclosure of key facts and figures to help buyers of securities make more informed judgments, and preventing the pyramiding and control of utilities through the device of the holding company.

In 1938, after these remedial actions had been legislated, Congress decided to launch a comprehensive inquiry into the causes of the economy's continued malfunctioning and the corrective actions that might be taken. The Temporary National Economic Committee (TNEC) was established by Congress and given a broad charter, considerable staff, and consulting help. Its work was not fully launched, however, when the growing clouds of World War II shifted the attention of Congress to more urgent defense matters. One of the early projects that was completed was a study by Gardiner Means presenting statistical evidence that large corporations were able to "administer" their prices. In other words, when demand fell they could restrict production and maintain prices, thereby interfering with the self-correcting tendencies of the market. Means' argument failed to persuade either his peers or the legislators.

The Modern Period of Analysis

The late thirties also saw the publication of R. H. Coase's seminal article, "The Nature of the Firm" (*Economica,* 1937). This article ushered in the modern period of analysis, in which economists and other social scientists took up the issue of organization that Marshall and Knight had earlier identified but not pursued. Coase asked a basic question: Why does a firm exist if, as most economists believe, the normal economic system works through the market? His answer was simple and direct: the impersonal price system entails hidden costs (the negotiation and enforcement of contracts), and economies can be achieved by avoiding market transactions. Coase, like Knight before him, saw important constraints on the growth of the firm stemming from the preferences and behavior of managers: there is a limit to how many subordinates a senior executive can effectively supervise; he might err in the allocation of resources at his command, which could give a competitor an edge; and finally, some able businessmen prefer autonomy to working for a corporation.

At about the time that Coase's article appeared, Chester I. Barnard, then president of New Jersey Bell, published his *The Functions of the Executive* (1938). Barnard addressed such questions as the nature of authority in a large organization; how incentives can be aligned to accomplish corporate objectives; the scope and limits of rules and regulations; and the nature and role of "informal organization." Barnard's approach was first and foremost that of a structuralist who sought to explain how the major divisions of a large organization are able to dovetail their operations to achieve corporate goals. He stated that tradition and personal relations softened formal organization policies and gave middle managers room within which to act and react.

In the middle of World War II, the Austrian-born Harvard economist Joseph Schumpeter published his challenging book, *Capitalism, Socialism and Democracy* (1942). In it he returned to a theme that had engaged his attention at the start of his career—the role of entrepreneurship in economic development. The mature Schumpeter reaffirmed and elaborated his earlier thesis that entrepreneurship is the prime mover of the economic process which, he noted, is a process of "creative destruction. The function of entrepreneurs is to reform and revolutionize the

Economists and the Corporation

pattern of production. . . . [Entrepreneurship] consists of getting things done" (p. 132).

Schumpeter believed, however, that this unique role of the entrepreneur and entrepreneurship was being undermined by scale and specialization. "Technological progress is increasingly becoming the business of teams of trained specialists. . . . Thus economic progress tends to become depersonalized and automatized. Business and committee work tends to replace individual action" (p. 133). In sum, Schumpeter believed that "the perfectly bureaucratized giant industrial unit not only ousts the small and medium-sized firm . . . but in the end also ousts the entrepreneur . . ." (p. 134). Important as it was, the further elaboration of Schumpeter's thesis had to wait for a quarter of a century until John K. Galbraith returned to this theme of how in the large corporation the R&D function becomes internalized and routinized (*The New Industrial State,* 1971).

In the intervening period there were several additional contributors to the emerging theory of the firm. The first was Herbert Simon, a psychologist, who went on to win the Nobel Prize in economics in 1978. His first important work, closely related to that of Chester Barnard, addressed issues under the rubric of *Administrative Behavior* (1947). His research interests took him far afield, and by the mid-1950s he had challenged conventional economists on two major fronts.

The classical model, with which most economists continued to work, assumed that the decision maker had sufficient information at his disposal to assess all possible alternatives and therefore could find the solution that would maximize his gains. But in the real world, Simon pointed out, information is always less than perfect and can be increased only through expenditures of time and money. Hence, decision making takes place in a world of *bounded rationality.*

Further, economists often postulated a unique set of goals and objectives acceptable to all members in the corporate hierarchy.

Yet the large corporation, Simon insisted, consists of many different groups with different interests; and a realistic approach must take into account the differences in goals between those at the top and those lower in the hierarchy.

Simon emphasized that a realistic approach to the decision-making process in a large organization must differentiate three distinct phases: finding occasions for making decisions, finding possible courses of action, and choosing among courses of actions. Differences in decision-making environments can explain how two comparable corporations, facing the same external conditions, may choose quite different strategies—one successful, the other leading to losses or even bankruptcy. Simon chides economists for their lack of attention to the internal operations of the firm. Internal decisions, he is convinced, are critical for understanding the dynamics of organizational performance and therefore much of what transpires in the economy at large.

Economist Harvey Leibenstein of Harvard University concurs with the assessment of Herbert Simon and his colleagues at Carnegie-Mellon about the importance of studying intraorganizational processes. Leibenstein notes that contemporary economists such as Scitovsky, Baumol, Maris, and Williamson have contributed to our understanding of the specific goals that managers seek to maximize—profit, sales, growth rate, and managerial prerogatives. But he stresses that one cannot ascribe to groups behavior that is descriptive only of individuals. Leibenstein asks outright, "What meaning can we give to the notion of maximizing utility of a group of individuals?" Although those at the top have the power to resolve conflicts, there is no basis for believing that their resolution will result in "joint maximization." Leibenstein's X-efficiency theory calls attention to the considerable latitude that managers in large organizations have to put forth more or less effort, the lack of pressure on most large corporations to push their costs to a minimum, and the strong tendency that exists toward organizational entropy. In short, Leibenstein has sought to persuade his fellow economists, with only limited success, that application of their central concepts of rationality and profit maximization to the internal operations of large corporations, characterized as they are by discrete groups with discrete goals, would lead to outcomes at variance with their assumptions about what happens in the marketplace, namely, maximum output with the most economical use of inputs.

Belatedly but surely, mainline economists, starting with Coase, have paid increasing attention to the gap between the basic postulates of neoclassical theory—namely, profit maximization under conditions of certainty—and the realities of modern corporate enterprise operating in a world of bounded rationality, with many different individuals and groups participating in decision making.

Economists have also made progress in characterizing both the conditions favoring continued reliance on the marketplace to achieve an optimal outcome and the conditions under which coordination within the firm may result in greater efficiencies. Kenneth Arrow, among others, has called attention to a number of instances of market failure with associated high costs, which shift the margin in favor of internalizing particular functions rather than relying on the market. On the other hand, a number of forces within the corporation may limit internal coordination. These run the gamut—from faulty investments to the preferences of many managers for a peaceful existence.

Galbraith, with a debt to Veblen and Schumpeter, believes that most of the barriers to internalization have been resolved through two basic adaptations. First, the large corporation has freed itself from the imperatives of the marketplace by relying on its own internal planning mechanism rather than on price signals. The major firms are big enough and strong enough to determine what to invest in, when to bring out new or improved products, and how to price them, without concern for the behavior of competitors.

Moreover, whatever the distribution of titles, power, and

rewards, the reality of corporate life and decision making, according to Galbraith, has become centered in the "techno-structure." This comprises an array of specialists in middle management responsible for developing the information, plans, and projects on which the future profitability of the corporation depends. Galbraith's focus on the important role of middle managers in shaping corporate strategy met with the approval of many of his colleagues and critics. His postulate that the large corporation, through internal planning, has freed itself from the dictates of the market, however, has not.

Current Views

Almost a century has passed since Marshall identified management as the fourth factor of production. And almost a half-century has passed since Coase demonstrated that the existence and growth of firms are linked to their ability to perform certain functions better than the market. Where does the theory of the firm now stand?

The prevailing view of the firm, best elaborated by Alfred Chandler, the leading historian of the large corporation (*The Visible Hand,* 1977), is a favorable one. *Fortune* 500 companies are adjusting their organizational structures and decision-making mechanisms to respond more effectively to the changes in the marketplace arising out of scale, diversity, technological progress, and internationalization. As the CEO of one of these companies remarked, those who adjust remain around and the others disappear. Reinforcement for such a benign evolutionary interpretation comes from the Chicago school of economists, who are convinced that the competitive market continues to dominate and only those firms that heed its signals survive. And Oliver Williamson, in his important December 1981 article in the *Journal of Economic Literature,* "The Modern Corporation:

Economists and the Corporation

Origins, Evolution, and Attributes," also views the continued growth and profitability of the large corporation as proof of its functionality and efficiency.

However, the concepts of survival and growth are gross categories. They hide almost as much as they disclose about the number of companies that succeed and fail; the length of time that companies are at or close to the top; the conditions that lead to their decline; and the factors explaining the exceptional corporation that is able to retain a position of dominance over decades. Moreover, the major concern of modern economists, when they finally began to study the corporation, has been with assessing the conditions that favor internal coordination versus recourse to the market; they have said little about the factors within the corporation that affect the quality of performance in the short and long term.

To the extent that economists have addressed our question—of how corporate structure affects the utilization of managerial personnel and, ultimately, the long-term prospects of the large corporation—they have given us two contrasting messages. One message is positive, the other negative, and occasionally both messages come from the same person.

The optimistic message is that the large corporation has been and is a major instrument for economizing the use of scarce entrepreneurial talent. The corporation speeds economic growth by enabling the great captains of industry to have an impact on a broader sector of the market, at home and abroad. Were it not for the evolution of the large corporation, the economies of scale in production and distribution would never have been realized because of the bottleneck in management. The large corporation eliminated this bottleneck. This is the upbeat message that was transmitted from Marshall to Knight, Coase, Schumpeter, Galbraith, and Chandler, a message that until recently was accepted doctrine. Overwhelmingly their message has been positive, although the first three called attention to some potential dangers: as executives age they often lose some of their energy;

scale can interfere with the CEO's knowing and judging his subordinates; a budding entrepreneur may prefer to work for himself rather than for a large company. However, the long line of skeptics and critics, from Adam Smith to Herbert Simon, has raised warnings. Simply stated, the economies of scale that the large corporation facilitates can be erased by the diseconomies of coordination and waste that are inherent in its operations. We will briefly recapitulate these negative appraisals of the large corporation's organization and decision-making functions. The point of this exercise is twofold: to indicate that the central theme of this book did not spring full-blown from our imagination but has roots that go back many years. Secondly, the insights of our predecessors provide a type of launching pad for our own work.

Summary

Adam Smith noted that when the owners of a business relied on professional directors to run it, the decisions taken would not necessarily result in optimal returns for the owners. Owners and managers might have conflicting objectives. In addition, the owners or directors of large corporations with worldwide operations would have difficulty getting subsidiary managers to adhere strictly to company policies and practices. In the absence of managerial conformity, not only would profits decline but serious breaches of discipline could endanger the future of the enterprise.

Marshall, despite his essentially favorable viewpoint, called attention to the effect of time on the fortunes of large successful companies. As the chief executive aged, he would not be as sharp and as energetic as he had been in his prime; and even if the company went public, there might be signs of slowdown because established institutions tend to lose some of their flexibility and speed of response.

More recent contributions to the theory of the firm have centered around the interactions between corporate scale and entrepreneurship and the quality of managerial performance. One line of argument promoted by Knight, Coase, Schumpeter, and Galbraith is that the large corporation has been able to economize in the use of entrepreneurial talent, the scarcest of all resources, precisely because of its size and complexity. A second line of argument, less optimistic in its conclusions, is presented by Simon and Leibenstein, who stress that the structural complexities of corporate life must be recognized as independent factors in assessing managerial behavior and outcomes. They see no basis in logic or in fact for projecting onto the large corporation the simplifying traditional assumption that all businessmen seek to maximize profits.

Finally there is an upbeat message from the functionalists— Chandler, Williamson, and the economists of the Chicago school—who believe that the market will continue to perform its classic function of providing challenges to the large corporation as much as to the small firm. Those firms that adapt to the market will be able to earn profits and survive; those that fail to do so will go under—a discipline that the market exerts on large and small alike.

But the predominant view among economists on the impact of scale is that there are no *a priori* limits. Since structure can be modified to accommodate to very large scale—at the extreme to exercise unified control over $100 billion of assets—it would be presumptuous and wrong to set a limit on the growth of the corporation.

There is a nagging realization among some of the economists who have looked hard at the large corporation that scale may have adverse impacts on managerial performance. Yet even these economists do not argue that the effects of scale on human resources could be so adverse as to jeopardize the corporation's future growth and profitability. Their strictures are more constrained; they point to a possible shortfall from maximum profits, but not to anything more.

Since the subject of corporate scale and managerial performance has never been at the center of their interest, it is not surprising that economists have neglected the implications of the corporate scale–human resources nexus. This nexus is much more significant under the present circumstances of heightened economic volatility and rapid change in the characteristics of corporate employees. But each of these facets is relevant and will command our attention as we seek additional perspectives.

In sum, in their analyses of the large corporation, economists have stressed the economies that accompany scale. Our point of departure is to acknowledge these economies but to focus on the diseconomies of coordination.

4

The Golden Age
and Later

Organizational changes in the modern corporation have come largely in response to changes in the economy. One way to expand and deepen our understanding of the ways in which large corporations have modified their organization to speed their growth and to assess the impact of these modifications on their use of managerial personnel is to look at the historical trend.

A review of the changes in corporate structure restricted to the years since the end of World War II would cover almost four decades. But, to put this postwar period into perspective, we must go back at least briefly to the New Era (1922–1929) and to the Great Depression and its aftermath (1929–1940).

Thus, we will discuss six decades, which we divide into three periods: the New Era plus the Depression and the subsequent years through the end of World War II (1922–1945); the postwar expansion, from 1945 to 1965; and the period of increasing volatility that began in the mid-sixties and still continues. In each of these periods, large U.S. corporations faced different sets of challenges and opportunities, which led them to modify, adjust, and change their organizational structures and modes of operation. Another critical dimension concerns the reciprocal impact on the corporation of changes in the number, types, and quality of their employees, particularly those who joined the managerial ranks; how they were in turn affected by the corporate environment is the theme of the next chapter.

The Depression and World War II

By the start of the New Era, the large manufacturing company was increasingly dominating the industrial landscape in the United States. Many of today's corporate leaders were already well entrenched: General Motors and Ford, General Electric and Westinghouse, Kodak, U.S. Steel, International Harvester, Goodyear, Firestone, and many more. At that time the U.S. market had reached a uniquely advanced stage of economic development: in the USSR Stalin was still engaged in consolidating his power, but the U.S. was a huge market in which a high proportion of families had considerable discretionary income. This unique circumstance encouraged manufacturers to hone their mass production techniques in order to reduce their unit costs—the surest way of capturing and holding a large share of the market.

Once ensconced, these large corporations had considerable protection against newcomers, who could challenge them only if they commanded large resources. It was conventional wisdom in the 1920s that with annual changes in models requiring large capital investments, no new company was likely to enter the automobile market. The continued dominance of the large manufacturing company, which had mastered the technique of mass producing goods that the American consumer needed or wanted, appeared assured. Small wonder that the world came to recognize the United States as the leader of mass production. No other country had such a sizable domestic market, such immense resources, or such efficient large corporations.

The human resources correlates of this leadership position rested on aggressive managers, some of whom were the founders or descendants of founders, a relatively large supply of engineering talent, a weak trade union movement that did not fear new technology, and a noninterfering government.

Nomenclature provides a clue to the basic optimism that informed industry and the nation in the 1920s. The New Era got its name from the belief that cyclical movements of business, with busts following booms and booms emerging out of busts, had come to an end. Many contemporary observers believed that the country had entered an era of "perpetual prosperity." Consequently, the collapse of the economy that followed the stock market break in October 1929 and the deep depression that followed was doubly traumatic. By 1933, gross national product had declined by about 30 percent in real terms from its 1929 high, unemployment was above 25 percent, agriculture was at such a low ebb that certain communities threatened to hang sheriffs who tried to sell off the property of defaulting owners. On the day that Roosevelt took the oath of office as president— March 4, 1933—all the nation's banks were closed.

The strenuous efforts that President Roosevelt and Congress initiated to reinvigorate the economy achieved considerable success. The downward spiral was brought to a halt, and the economy began to expand and continued for the next several years on an upward course. Even so, eleven years after the onset of the depression, in 1940, unemployment was still above 10 percent and the GNP had not regained its 1929 level. Moreover, the New Deal had changed the rules of the game. Not only had the federal government interposed itself as a major player, but Roosevelt, in rewarding his supporters and solidifying his political base, had done a great deal to strengthen the trade union movement. For the first time the unions had become established in the heartland of the U.S. economy—in automobiles, steel, rubber, chemicals, and other leading industries.

After 1933, much of the time, energy, and attention of corporate leaders was directed to learning to live in this new environment, in which government and labor individually and jointly were engaged in seeking to take power away from the owners and managers of capital. In this period of continuing low demand, straitened balance sheets, and repeated disappointments with the speed of the recovery, most large companies moved cautiously. They sought to conserve cash, keeping tight control over new hires and promotions, and avoiding actions that would reduce their future flexibility. They also sought to slow the growth of union power, which they perceived as a threat to their management prerogatives and future profitability.

Despite ten years of lackluster performance with little innovation and less restructuring, American corporations were able, in 1940, to respond strongly when the nation decided to mobilize and gear up for war. The conversion to a war economy made demands on the nation's corporations that drew on their long-term strength—the mass production of standard output. Airplanes, tanks, ships, guns, ammunition and much more were produced in prodigious quantities within tight time schedules. As some of the president's more farsighted advisers realized, the potential danger lay not in the inability of American industry to respond but in the government's setting its requirements too low.

Fortunately, Roosevelt sided with the optimists, and American industry not only met but often exceeded the high targets that had been set. These impressive production goals were achieved despite large losses of managerial personnel, who entered government service in civilian or military roles. Corporations also had to find replacements, often from among women and minorities, for the many skilled workers and operatives who enlisted or were drafted for military service. Despite the attendant stress and strain, and the concomitant shifts in products and personnel, corporate performance was outstanding.

The Postwar Boom

When the war ended, most economists and government officials felt the country would face a return to high levels of unemployment. But the Committee for Economic Development, established under the leadership of Paul Hoffman, made an important contribution to forestall this by alerting businessmen to the importance of quickly initiating plans for reconversion.

At the beginning of 1945 a group of senior government economists and a few other specialists spent an evening in Washington, D.C., discussing the job outlook after the cessation of hostilities. Almost without exception they anticipated a speedy return to the high levels of unemployment existing in 1940. When Benjamin V. Cohen expressed doubts about this view, he was joined by only one other person—a betting man who said that if the overwhelming number of his colleagues anticipated a particular outcome, he would on principle take the opposite position and anticipate that the economy would make the transition to peace without experiencing a new spell of high unemployment.

The reconversion at war's end, in the second half of 1945 and in 1946, was truly remarkable. Factories often had to be turned completely around. Many wartime employees, especially younger women, left to marry or to start families. Many managers and skilled workmen on war leave decided not to return to their former companies but sought new positions. Ten million soldiers and sailors were demobilized and, while some entered school and others took some time off, most sought jobs and were quickly reabsorbed.

At war's end, American business was looking at a market with a pent-up demand for goods of all kinds—from new automobiles, which had not been available to civilians for five years, to new construction, which had been at a low ebb for more than fifteen years. American corporations were once again able to draw on their strength, which was to turn out quickly a great volume of standard products that the consumer needed and wanted. And the consumer had large accumulated savings which he was eager to spend.

The war had left its mark on many senior and middle managers. Many took pride in having been part of a winning military team. Moreover, they had been impressed by several aspects of the military: staff-line organization; planning and control units; schools for management development; and advanced personnel techniques for recruiting, assignment, and evaluation. They had learned firsthand what a well-structured organization could accomplish in large-scale movements of people and supplies, logistical lessons that they carried back with them to their companies. The war and postwar relocation of population within the United States, from east to west, from rural to urban, out of poverty areas in the South, strengthened the postwar economy and provided many business enterprises with an opportunity to transform themselves from local and regional entities into national companies.

Many large corporations, recognizing the advantages of proximity to the consumer, moved to control and expand their distribution channels and also branched out in other directions by providing financing and other services. They were thus able to integrate more efficiently their production and inventories with final sales. This integration helped them to cut costs and add to their profits, and it also enabled them to tie the consumer yet more closely to them, an advantage when it came to future sales.

The Golden Age and Later

The transformation of many local and regional companies into national corporations and their success at forward (and sometimes backward) integration facilitated (and was facilitated in many cases by) their change from single into multiproduct companies. These developments, together with direct control over distribution channels, required significant adjustments in both organizational structures and human resources policies. On the organizational front, corporations moved to decentralize and divisionalize. At the same time they added planning and control staffs to their expanding headquarters, as well as lower-level staff that were responsible for keeping tabs on the rapidly expanding divisions. In the early years of the post–World War II era, the rate of growth of the more successful corporations was often so rapid that the newly expanded staffs had a difficult time just keeping up with and recording the monthly and quarterly gains that were being achieved.

On the human resources front the GI Bill of Rights enabled many veterans to complete their interrupted studies and encouraged many others to reopen their educational and career plans. During the immediate postwar years, there was an increased output of college graduates, many of whom found positions in the expanding corporations in manufacturing, marketing, or staff functions.

By about 1948 or 1949 the immediate postwar hunger for goods had essentially been met. Most companies understood that continued profitability and growth would now depend on their success in expanding sales both at home and especially abroad, where they had begun to operate. Consequently they began to pay more attention to this phase of their business. They knew how to produce. They had little difficulty making what they were able to sell. So they concentrated on selling.

As the 1950s progressed, the growing strength of unions also became a matter of concern. If a strike occurred and was not quickly settled, the company risked losing its market share to competitors. To protect the continuity of production and the company's market share became the primary task of corporate industrial relations specialists. Nonunionized companies devoted considerable managerial time and effort to keeping the unions out. The more profitable of these companies were willing to pay for their continued freedom by offering higher wages and better fringe benefits.

The other principal human resources issues revolved around the recruitment, assignment, and career development of the many junior executives who were being hired straight out of college and business school to fill the new positions in sales and sales-related areas as well as the proliferating staff functions. The large companies were able to trade on the desire of these young people for job security and an opportunity to advance up the corporate ladder. In extending an initial offer of employment, corporations made it clear that if the newly hired graduate did well, he could look forward to a lifetime career with valuable benefits including a liberal pension. And the desire of many trainees to move ahead quickly could be met because these rapidly expanding corporations continually needed to fill management positions at headquarters, in the field, and, later, overseas. During their military service many young executives had become accustomed to frequent changes in location. The fact that their wives were busy rearing two, three, or more children, and the willingness of most large corporations to assume the responsibility and costs of moving their household effects, led to the creation of a highly mobile group of young executives who were on the fast track.

In general, this was a period of rapid change in internal organization. As mentioned, senior executives often adapted for corporate use much of what they had learned in the military about setting organizational goals, strategic planning, management development, and organizational morale. Many companies made substantial investments in both internal and external training for middle managers who were judged to have potential for promotion. At the same time, corporate staff worked hard to develop and codify corporate policies and procedures that would guide managers in acting and reacting to problems and challenges from within and from the outside. These organizational specialists, and the top managers to whom they reported, realized that a large organization could function effectively only if those down the line knew the rules and were conditioned to follow them.

The U.S. economy dominated the international scene during the first two decades following the end of World War II. Bretton Woods established the dollar as the world's principal currency. The United States, through its welfare and rehabilitation programs, including the Marshall Plan, obtained a leading role in both Western Europe and Japan. Its control of the atomic bomb reinforced its political power and leverage. All of the foregoing helped the more aggressive U.S. corporations to become multinationals with important market niches on other continents. Their dominant role in the U.S. market provided them the springboard for their growth overseas.

During these two decades these large multinationals had little to fear from Germany or other European competitors and even less from the Japanese, who had not previously penetrated the U.S. market. These countries were busy rebuilding their war-devastated economies. As they progressed, their export trade gradually revived but was at first directed to countries other than the United States.

The U.S. multinationals soon gained confidence that they could grow rapidly while maintaining control over their diversified operations. As Europe began to recover from the devastation of World War II and to expand at a respectable rate, many U.S. companies decided that it would be wise to establish a presence there before the European Economic Community erected barriers to keep them out. These large U.S. companies had a clear advantage at this point. They knew how to efficiently mass produce consumer-durable products, ranging from automobiles to refrigerators, which were in demand by the growing number of European consumers who could afford them. And these U.S.

corporations had become increasingly proficient in linking their production to the market. Moreover, R&D-based companies soon realized that because Europeans lagged behind on the technology front, it was possible to market abroad processes and products that had exhausted their high earnings potential in the United States. Put simply, many U.S. corporations were able to obtain abroad a second return on their investments. Finally, they were confident that they had mastered the organizational and human resources challenges required to manage large international enterprises.

Small wonder, therefore, that some perceptive European observers concluded in the late 1950s and early 1960s that these large American companies were well on their way to dominating the European economy and before long would be in effective control of Europe's economic destiny. Prior to 1965, the post–World War II track record of the leading U.S. companies was so strong that many Europeans believed, from what they read in their own press and in the American press, that these companies had developed unique organizational structures and management techniques that accounted for their remarkable success. Accordingly, they sent increasing numbers of their best students to study at leading graduate schools of business in the United States, in the hope that after mastering the new management techniques, they could upon their return help to modernize lagging European enterprises.

In retrospect, it appears that the good track record of many large U.S. corporations can be explained mainly by their long-term experience in mass production and their postwar successes in meshing their production with sales. Innovations—whether in organizational structure, human resources policies, technology, or new product development—seem to have played a lesser role, although significant exceptions to this broad generalization do exist. Without minimizing their accomplishments, we believe that these U.S. multinationals had the great good fortune to be spared strong foreign competition at home until the 1960s.

The Golden Age and Later

Moreover, they had the many advantages of having established a presence in Western Europe and in the Third World, aided by the strength of the dollar and the indirect benefits from large U.S. military and foreign aid programs.

The Turbulent Environment

The third period, which began in the mid-sixties, has been characterized by growing volatility. If external factors had previously helped the large U.S. corporation to succeed, they now turned negative. Once the international economic environment became turbulent, the corporation's organizational structures and human resources policies were no longer able to effectively respond.

By the mid-sixties, West Germany and Japan had emerged as major competitors in the world's markets, as had many other nations including France, Italy, the Netherlands, Sweden, and smaller Asian countries and territories such as Taiwan, Malaysia, Hong Kong, and South Korea. To differing extents, each of these countries had begun to nibble at one or more of the lucrative markets in the United States or in other parts of the world where previously U.S. corporations had the field largely to themselves.

A parallel development coming at the end of these two decades of rapid expansion was the change in the tastes and behavior of the American consumer. After repeated large-scale purchases of consumer durables, from refrigerators to automobiles, the U.S. buying public had become surfeited with standard products. The steady rise in family income, accelerated by the growth of the two-worker family, increased the consumers' disposable income to a point where they could afford to indulge new tastes for novelty, quality, and service. The increase in the sales of foreign cars and Japanese electronic products reflected the growing responsiveness of the U.S. consumer to quality goods.

As the economy of the United States and, later, Western Europe and Japan expanded in the 1950s and 1960s, wage rates and fringe benefits also increased. Employers producing standard goods that require a heavy labor input began to look for alternative production sites. Some West European as well as U.S. companies found these sites in low-wage areas such as Mexico and Spain, while others established plants in the Far East, Hong Kong, Taiwan, Singapore, and Malaysia. Swedish and Dutch industrialists, much more dependent than U.S. corporations on exports, realized that the world economy was entering a new era that was likely to unsettle many long-established and profitable companies, particularly in Western Europe. As early as 1970, some Swedish business leaders took seriously the threat that within a decade they might no longer be able to manufacture in Sweden for export but would have to relocate their plants in low-wage countries. This did not occur to nearly the extent that they had feared. But by the early 1970s, Philips, headquartered at Einhoven, the Netherlands, was well advanced in setting up multiple manufacturing units in Southeast Asia, a move later imitated by many other multinationals.

The Japanese, who were faced with a slow-growing labor force at home and unwilling to follow the West European practice of using guest workers, were probably the first advanced manufacturing country to seek out low-wage, off-shore locations. By 1970 a major Japanese electronics concern was leaving Hong Kong and Taiwan, where wage rates had risen rapidly, was expanding in Malaysia, and was looking at Thailand for future sites.

Other factors added to the problems of the U.S. corporation. When West Germany and Japan reentered the world markets, they did so with modern plants and the most advanced equipment. Their factories had been turned into rubble by bombs and fire, and they had had no option but to rebuild from the ground up. Many U.S. companies, on the other hand, had become accustomed, during the prolonged period when they had the market largely to themselves, to making do with old plants and often with aging equipment. By the mid-1960s, they were being outdistanced by competitors who had leapfrogged them on the technological front.

Additional difficulties stemmed from uncritical projection of the growth and profit records that were being achieved both at home and abroad in the early postwar years. Once Europe and Japan recovered and reentered the market, the U.S. multinationals were certain to confront a more competitive environment. Other large U.S. corporations had the domestic market largely to themselves and were able to earn profits by using aging plants and outmoded equipment. In the absence of strong competition from abroad, many felt little pressure to make heavy investments in state of the art technology. But as the international competition intensified and imports into the United States increased, many U.S. companies could no longer profit from their long-protected position.

We noted earlier that marketing and sales had increasingly engaged the attention of senior U.S. management during the post–World War II expansion. Accordingly, these functions attracted much of the capital and scarce talent. Many corporations acted as if manufacturing could take care of itself, requiring little attention from senior executives. In time, this message was so clear that fewer and fewer of the talented recruits opted for a manufacturing position. In fact, many engineers who had started out in manufacturing and did well quickly sought an opportunity to shift into sales or general management, where salaries were higher and opportunities greater.

To add to these distortions, many U.S. corporations, especially those that had to contend with strong unions, often pursued labor relations policies that reduced their future flexibility. They agreed to changes in work rules that limited their managerial prerogatives, preferring them to larger wage settlements that included additional wage or bonus payments or more paid holidays. Or they agreed to high wage settlements in order to avoid a strike, on the assumption that they could pass most or all of the additional cost onto the consumer. As long as strong competitors were not in the market or on the horizon, such a strategy could be justified. But when at first a few and later more competitors, many from abroad, did appear, the earlier strategy of a live-and-let-live relationship with their unions greatly reduced the corporations' capacity to respond aggressively to the market.

The acceleration of hostilities in Vietnam and the concomitant stimulation of defense industries camouflaged for a time the growing weakness of the U.S. economy. There were, however, a number of signals: the rise in inflation, the weakening of the dollar, mounting federal deficits, and an unfavorable balance of trade. In August 1971, President Nixon had no option but to end the free conversion of the U.S. dollar into gold.

Nixon's action had many characteristics of a "force majeure." The long-established Bretton Woods agreement on stable exchange rates had been strained to the breaking point, and there was no quick way to put an alternative arrangement in place. Moreover, many of the world's leading economists favored floating exchange rates that would follow upon the end to dollar convertibility.

The simultaneity of the 1972 boom among most of the advanced economies led to steep advances in commodity prices, and in 1973 the first oil crisis put OPEC in control. The stage was set for the long postwar expansion to come to an end, and come to an end it did.

At the same time inflation accelerated. Keynesian economic policies, which had helped European countries operate with 1 to 2 percent unemployment, were no longer practical. Interest rates, even when corrected for inflation, climbed rapidly, and both the United States and the Common Market countries were caught up in an increasingly volatile environment. Only Japan succeeded in maintaining a relatively strong expansionary course.

In the years after 1973, the combination of much slower economic growth, rising unemployment, and rampant inflation led to an increased level of political interventions in the international economic sphere. The wide range of responses includes U.S. and European pressures on Japan for voluntary restrictions on exports, the U.S. embargo on grain to the U.S.S.R., the temporary breach in economic relations between Organization for Economic Cooperation and Development [OECD] nations and Argentina, and the intensified difficulties between the United States and its allies over the construction of the natural gas pipeline from the U.S.S.R. to Western Europe. As of this writing, the underlying international structure of trade relations is under increasing pressure, with some experts voicing the fear that the cumulative breaches might soon bring the era of "free trade" to an end.

In the late 1960s and again in the late 1970s a rash of mergers and acquisitions took place in the United States, leading to the emergence of new large conglomerates. Primarily, older manufacturing concerns acquired units that specialized in financial and other services. While the precipitating factors differed, the trend was sped by the belief among U.S. business leaders that they had mastered the problems of running large diversified organizations. They concluded that decentralization, divisionalization, and strong central staff enabled them to make the essential strategic decisions that they could not delegate. With strong information and control systems in place, the chief executive of a large conglomerate and his senior associates would be able to keep the organization headed in the right direction and profitable.

The prototypical conglomerator in the 1960s was Harold Geneen of ITT. With the backing of the investment banker André Mayer of Lazard Freres, Geneen (see *Financier* by Cary Reich, 1983), accomplished a series of interrelated objectives: to restructure the market on which ITT depended for most of its sales from overseas to the United States; to increase the scale of its revenues and profits; to diversify out of telecommunications and electronics; and finally, to demonstrate that a highly diversified company could be successfully managed through tight controls that included monthly review of managerial accomplishments with the aid of data produced by internal accounting systems.

The rise of conglomerates depends in the first instance on the mood and behavior of the stock market. During much of the 1960s, it was favorable to acquisitions, many of which occurred through exchanges of stock. Whether the acquiring company gained a great deal, a little, or eventually nothing depended on how much it had to pay for the acquisition, whether its estimates of market trends turned out to be correct and, most important, whether it was able to realize the potential of the acquired company by either retaining the old management or replacing it with an effective new team. Few owner-managers are willing to remain at the head of an acquired company after it has been absorbed because, among other reasons, future strategic decisions are no longer theirs to make. Some agree to remain for a while but soon find the new corporate constraints disagreeable and leave. But, as many conglomerates have discovered, putting their own managers, most of whom lack experience in the acquired company's area of expertise, generally does not work. For this very reason, after a few years of disappointing results, many acquired companies have been sold, often at a loss.

Profitable corporations tend to retain earnings because their stockholders want to avoid paying taxes on their dividends and top management feels more secure with more assets under its control. But the assets have to be put to work. Few successful corporations have the breadth and depth of managerial personnel to staff new businesses and to provide the quality of leadership that will enable them to continue to grow and increase their profitability. The Achilles' heel of many mergers, then, is the fact that the old management is replaced by corporate managers who lack the background and knowledge of the new business and its markets. This is one more illustration of where scale and human resources are out of sync.

The Golden Age and Later

Mergers and acquisitions helped account for the increasing importance of the finance office at the top echelon of most large corporations. The growing amounts of accumulated cash and short-term assets as well as the greater complexities of operating in foreign exchange markets were also factors. In the past, corporations had relied much more on their commercial and investment bankers.

The implications of volatile markets in foreign exchange are suggested in *Exxon Corporation 1983 Annual Report,* which states that "foreign exchange losses included in determining net income totaled $107 million in 1982 and $56 million in 1983. The decrease in stockholder's equity in these two years from exchange rate changes amounted to $819 million and $539 million respectively."

The professional managers who now occupy the top positions in the corporate world are measured and measure themselves primarily by three criteria: growth in the corporation's share of the market; the trend in earnings per share; and the price of the company's stock. In fact, these criteria played an important role in stimulating the merger and acquisition movements in the late 1960s and the late 1970s. And their implications extend far beyond this arena. These criteria have tended to favor decisions based on short- and intermediate-term financial considerations rather than on long-term product innovation and market leadership.

The federal government, as noted earlier, contributed to establishing and maintaining an economic environment that facilitated the growth of the large corporation. Some additional dimensions of government policy had both a supportive and unsettling impact on the business environment. A large flow of federal funds for defense, space, and R&D created a large and profitable market for major aerospace companies. Many companies developed considerable skill in dealing with the federal government. But it was difficult for their own managements, and even more difficult for outside analysts, to reach sound judgments about how well they were currently performing and about the implications of large government contracts for their future growth and profitability. Some large contractors, recognizing this danger, made special efforts to keep their defense business apart from their commercial lines. They realized that they would not be able to compete and survive in the civilian marketplace unless they immunized themselves from the cost-plus method of contracting with the Department of Defense, in which they could usually cover large overruns through renegotiations.

The ongoing large-scale expenditures of the federal government, however, stimulated many defense contractors to enter new fields, to acquire additional expertise, to train large numbers of specialists, and to learn how to respond quickly to changing defense requirements. Some aerospace companies were led to experiment with interesting innovations in organizational structures and management styles. Some of these innovations turned out to have broad applicability for the civilian side of their business. Several of the nation's leading corporations, including AT&T, IBM, and General Electric, developed a high degree of sophistication in bidding on selected government contracts that had the potential of speeding their success in new and promising civilian markets.

This greatly enlarged role of government as a purchaser of defense and space products was paralleled by the sizable concurrent investments it made in higher education and research and development. Government money broadened and deepened the national research base and greatly enlarged the pool of specialists. An important by-product of governmental spending was the emergence of a new type of scientist-businessman, technologist-entrepreneur. Such individuals, by commingling venture capital with government contracts, were able to establish new firms specializing in the production of esoteric products based on R&D. This is the story of Silicon Valley in California and Route 128 near Boston.

The Golden Age and Later

Many of these new high-tech enterprises grew quickly into moderate-sized firms, but at that point they often encountered hurdles to further growth. Some were bought up by large corporations looking for opportunities to diversify. Others, after some good years, ran into trouble because of the loss of a major government contract or of key personnel, who, in many cases, emerged as competition. Most frequently, though, these firms were simply unable to manage the increasingly complex organizational, financial, and marketing changes that would have enabled them to continue growing.

These few observations about high-tech companies provide a point of contrast to the past successes and present tensions that afflict many of the multinationals. Through divisionalization, decentralization, and strong corporate staff, the multinationals were able to take advantage of burgeoning markets in the early post–World War II decades to expand significantly both their revenues and their profits. Although responsibility for many operating decisions was delegated to the field, critical decision-making power involving capital allocations, entrance into new markets, launching of new products, R&D funding, and even pricing tended to remain heavily concentrated in the hands of the senior executives. The hierarchical structure of the large corporation underwent few basic changes.

Conclusions

There is no gainsaying the fact that many large U.S. corporations grew from strength to strength in the period immediately following World War II. Only the explanation for their success is in dispute. The contemporary view, both in the United States and abroad, was that their excellent track record reflected their organizational skill in meeting and surmounting the challenges of increasing scale. In particular their well-honed personnel policies were able to identify, develop, and promote managers capable of functioning successfully in more demanding positions.

In fact, as we have seen, much of the large corporation's success was based on its effective integration of mass production with mass markets that were able and eager to absorb standardized products. Today, however, consumers place greater weight on novelty, quality, and customization. Meeting this change in consumer tastes is, then, one of the challenges that large corporations must face. More generally, they must face the challenge of operating in today's volatile markets in a world economy that is experiencing a much slower rate of growth.

Speedy adjustment to the changing market is one challenge. An even more important challenge, however, is internal. The structures and mechanisms that large corporations had developed earlier to motivate and direct the work of their managerial cadres and, especially, to dovetail the relations between managers in operating divisions and those at headquarters now appear wanting.

The competitive struggle is almost always played out in the marketplace but the winners and the losers are often foreshadowed by internal factors. A company can succeed only if it structures and maintains an internal environment that enables it to elicit the motivation, energy, and creativity of its managerial personnel. For it is their ideas and actions that largely determine its future growth and profitability. The years immediately following World War II were the Golden Age for large U.S. corporations because they had the market essentially to themselves. This fact hid shortcomings in both their organizational structures and their human resources policies. But in the more recent period of growing international economic volatility, these shortcomings have become more pronounced. Today they can no longer be ignored—not without placing these large corporations at risk.

5

The Changing
Human Resources
Pool

Corporate organization and structure make it possible for smaller or larger numbers of individuals to cooperate in performing a range of discrete tasks, the sum total of which enables the business enterprise to accomplish its specific goals. In the process of accomplishing these goals, the enterprise provides work and career opportunities for its members and dividends for its stockholders. Without organization, structure, and decision-making rules, no corporation can function. But it should be quickly added that organization alone is inert and incapable of acting or reacting. Only human beings can energize an enterprise and give it meaning and direction.

By the time they take their first job, most people have had twenty or so years of developmental experiences and education. This means that their values, attitudes, and behavior are already pretty well fixed. A sophisticated enterprise adapts its policies and procedures to this reality. But even a sophisticated corporation can stumble if it fails to make adjustments in its structure, decision-making, and human resources policies in the face of significant changes that have occurred in the labor pool.

The half century from 1930 to 1980 saw a great many changes in the values, education, and expectations of successive cohorts of corporate personnel who left their mark on the companies they joined. Unfortunately, most large corporations have been slow to alter their work assignments and reward structures to better fit the preferences of their employees, particularly those who have recently entered the managerial ranks.

Since corporate mangers are drawn primarily from among college and professional school graduates, we will focus on the expansion in the numbers of graduates and their areas of specialization. This perspective will help shed light on the hotly debated question of whether the United States is facing a shortage of technical personnel. The quantitative and qualitative changes that have occurred during the past half century can be summarized by considering the shifts in the industrial and occupational profiles of the U.S. economy, and by relating these shifts to the dominance of the large corporation, with its increasing reliance on educated personnel.

The Human Resources Pool: 1930

We start this account with 1930, the end of the New Era that had ushered in the automobile age and, with it, the first stage of suburbanization. Since the decade of the 1930s was an unrelieved period of suboptimal output, employment, and income, the end of the 1920s marks the high point in the pre–World War II performance of the economy.

Prior to the stock market crash in October 1929, U.S. manu-

The Changing Human Resources Pool

facturing commanded the admiration of the world. The United States was at the cutting edge of technology, well endowed with natural resources, protected by oceans on the east and west, with friendly neighbors on the north and south, and a domestic market of unparalleled size. The observers of the day, both at home and abroad, were also impressed with the fact that the United States had long recognized the importance of developing its human resources. It had taken the lead in creating a broad system of public education, open to all. It supported a great many colleges, which provided postsecondary educational opportunities to many qualified young men and women, especially those from middle-class families. And it had an impressive array of major universities, under nonprofit and state auspices.

And the United States possessed other advantages in human resources. Americans were considered to be "natural" mechanics, reflecting the fact that many had grown up on farms, where they were early exposed to machinery and its maintenance. As a nation of immigrants, the country had attracted many of the world's young, venturesome, and energetic individuals. In turn, its traditions and politics were supportive of individuals who sought to pursue money-making proclivities.

The workers who helped to propel the United States into a leadership role in mass production were drawn from two groups: the immigrants and their children and excess labor from the farms. These groups became the operatives and later the skilled workers for the expanding manufacturing firms. Large employers were also able to hire significant numbers of engineers and other scientific and technical personnel from among the graduates of the nation's colleges and universities.

But not all signs were positive. In 1924, the United States had moved to radically restrict its immigration quotas. Its black minority of about 12 million, accounting for just under 10 percent of the total population, lived primarily in the rural South, under social and economic conditions of segregation and widespread poverty. In other regions, the development and

95

utilization of the nation's human resources were often adversely affected by discrimination based on sex, ethnic origin, religion, and poverty.

The Changing Pool: 1930–1980

During the half century from 1930 to 1980, a series of momentous changes in the nation's human resources occurred. First, there was a large-scale growth in both the total population and the labor force. Second, the composition of the labor force was altered by the expanded participations in the world of work of women and minorities. Shifts in the origins and numbers of immigrants, also had an impact. Finally, there was a vast increase in educational and training institutions and in the number and qualifications of their graduates. Paralleling these changes were shifts in the nation's industries and occupations. The interactions among these several sets of changes radically transformed the nation's pool of human resources.

We will start with the growth in population. In 1930, the population stood at 123 million; in 1980 at 227 million. During this half century, then, the United States increased its population by over 100 million. In the first 140 years of the nation's history, from 1790 to 1930, the total increase had been only slightly greater. It is worth noting that during the past half century, the number of blacks in the population more than doubled, from under 12 million to over 26 million, or from 9.7 percent to 11.7 percent of the total.

Changes in the size of the population affect but do not determine changes in the number of adults who are willing and able to work. It is possible to have different employment/ population ratios (E/P), that is, the number in the labor force (at work or seeking work) as a proportion of the number of all adults (16 or older) who are not institutionalized. And in fact,

The Changing Human Resources Pool

the increase in the labor force from 50 million in 1930 to 107 million in 1980 was proportionately greater than the increase in the total adult population. Between 1947 and 1980, the E/P ratio rose from 58.9 to 65.3, or by more than 10 percent.

This substantial increase in the E/P ratio might seem remarkable given the fact that during the postwar period there were two developments that shortened the length of our working life and should have depressed the ratio. On the one hand, young people remained in school longer. (Prior to 1967 the U.S. Bureau of Labor Statistics had included fourteen- and fifteen-year-olds in counting individuals available for work.) On the other hand, more and more people stopped working at an earlier age. For instance, between 1948 and 1980 the labor force participation rate of males in the age group 55–64 declined from over 89 percent to 72 percent, or by about one-fifth; for those 65 or over, the decline was more precipitous, from 47 to 19 percent.

The primary explanation of this decline in the labor force participation of men, especially since their average span of life was increasing, was the improvement in their retirement income from Social Security, private pensions, and personal savings. The young elderly were better able to enjoy their leisure. The trend to early retirement also reflected the preference of large organizations to make room at and near the top for those lower in the hierarchy to move up.

The rise of E/P ratio during the post–World War II years, despite a strong movement to earlier retirement on the part of men, is explained by the revolutionary change in the participation of women in the world of work. Their participation rate increased from just under one-third (32.7 percent) in 1948 to over one-half in 1980 (51.6 percent). Absolute figures help to reinforce the magnitude of this change. In 1948 the total labor force, including the members of the armed forces, amounted to 62 million. In 1980 the total stood at 107 million, or 46 million more. Males accounted for 18 million of this increase, women for 28 million.

We use the term "revolutionary" since women accounted for 60 percent of all new job holders in the post–World War II era and most of the new women workers were married, many with young children at home. Prior to the war, white women, once they were married, did not generally enter paid employment out of the home. In fact, some states, such as Massachusetts, required that women workers (teachers and other civil servants) resign when they married.

In recent decades the United States has faced three major challenges on the employment front. It has had to accommodate the large numbers of older and, more recently, younger married women who want to work or keep on working after starting a family. Since the mid-1960s, it has had to expand the number of jobs to make room for the baby-boom cohort (1945–1959), which turned out to be twice as large as the preceding depression and war cohort (1930–1945). In the 1950s the number of young persons reaching working age each year was in the 2 million range; by the mid-1960s this figure had jumped to over 4 million. Finally, it has had to absorb the fluctuating but growing numbers of immigrants and refugees (over 10 million since 1950), and it has provided at least another 5 million jobs for illegal aliens.

How well the economy responded is suggested by the following. In 1960 about 66 million people held jobs in the civilian sector; in 1980 the figure was in excess of 97 million, an increase of 31 million. Within a single generation—20 years—the economy was able to increase its total number of jobs by 47 percent. Many of these new jobs paid relatively low wages and/or provided only part-time work, and not all those who wanted work could find it. But, overall, the U.S. economy responded well to meeting the expanded demand for jobs. Even during the sluggish 1970s, over 18 million new jobs were added. Despite this remarkable increase, the numbers and proportion of the unemployed rose substantially—from 4 million, or 5 percent, in 1970 to about 7.5 million, or 7 percent, in 1980 and about 11 million, or almost 11 percent, at the end of 1982. This trend

The Changing Human Resources Pool

was a consequence of the continuing increase in new job seekers and the softening demand for labor after 1979. The substantial improvement in the economy in 1983 was accompanied by a strengthening in the labor market. Thus unemployment dropped to around 8.5 percent late in 1983, fell below 8 percent early in 1984, and dropped to 7 percent by the end of the year.

This brief account of the quantitative changes in the population and labor force shows the critical relationship between the number of workers and the growth of the economy. If a larger proportion of the total population wants to work, the stage is set for an expansion in real output, in total as well as on a per capita basis. The potential will be transformed into reality, of course, only to the extent that the enlarged labor force is able to obtain productive employment. In the postwar period, the economy performed well, by providing such opportunities for most, if not all, who sought to work.

Qualitative Changes

The number of workers is only part of the human resources equation. Just as important are the skills and competences of those who are employed or looking for work. In this regard, the quantity and quality of prior education and training become critical. Comparisons between 1940 and 1980 show substantial increases in the educational preparation of the U.S. work force. The average years of schooling increased, as did the number and proportion of new entrants who had obtained a college or advanced degree.

In 1940 the median years of schooling completed by the entire population 25 years and older was 8.6 years. Most adults had dropped out by their first year in high school. Only 1 in every 4 had graduated from high school, and less than 1 in 20 was a college graduate or had earned a higher degree. The picture was radically different in 1980. Median school years completed had risen to 12.5 years, a gain of 45 percent. Almost 7 out of 10 adults had earned at least a high school diploma, and there had been an almost fourfold increase in the proportion of college and advanced degree holders, from 4.6 to 17 percent of the total population. Some believe that the foregoing provides too favorable a picture and needs to be adjusted for a decline in quality. But that decline is difficult to substantiate, especially in view of the marked improvement in teacher preparation and the lengthening of the school year.

Whenever a society is undergoing radical change, averages that include the entire population often mask the extent of the change. The best way to avoid the dead weight of the past is to consider comparisons between the younger age groups. Today only 1 in 7 in the 25–29 age group has not completed high school. Close to 1 in 4 is a college graduate or has acquired a higher degree.

The most remarkable gains in recent decades have been achieved by blacks. In 1940, more than 4 out of every 10 blacks had completed less than five years of schooling, the standard of "functional literacy" used by the armed services during World War II. Only 1 in 14 was a high school graduate, and about 1 in 75 had earned a college degree. In 1980, among the younger cohort of blacks (25 to 29 years of age) less than 1 percent had failed to complete five years of schooling. More than 3 out of 4 had obtained high school diplomas, and about 1 in 8 had obtained a college or higher degree.

This "catching-up" phenomenon must not minimize or deny the fact that many black youths attending inner-city schools are not obtaining the educational qualifications they need to obtain a job, especially a job with prospects. But it does mean that the large educational gap between whites and blacks has been significantly narrowed.

Americans prize education for a variety of reasons—religious, social, economic, and cultural. The Puritans wanted to be sure that their offspring could read and study the Bible. Then, when non–English-speaking immigrants arrived in droves, it was essential for social harmony and nation building that as many children as possible receive the benefits of schooling. As early as the Civil War, Congress had recognized that higher education was crucial for the development of agriculture and industry, and had taken action to support it. And in recent years education has been perceived as a way of broadening the individual's horizon and providing the entire citizenry with the intellectual tools to extract more meaning and value out of life.

But the economic (vocational) value of education has always been at the fore. Americans have always asked whether education pays and have looked to the labor market for the answer. The statistics point to the close ties between educational level and median income. At the end of the 1970s the median income of persons who reported income was $12,500: people with less than 8 years of education earned $5,900; those with 1 to 3 years of high school, $9,100; high school graduates, $13,300; and individuals with postgraduate degrees, $22,800. While this crude measure requires refinement, especially to reflect age and full- versus part-time participation in the labor force, the spread between different levels of educational achievement and median earnings would be sustained.

After the end of World War II, most families seemed to place greater value on education. For example, they no longer expected their unmarried children to cover or even contribute to meeting their expenses while they continued to live at home. Older children were no longer an economic asset, since after graduating from high school many required assistance from their families to continue their education. Many married women went to work to help put one or more children through college. In the past, children had often contributed to the family income after leaving high school. The taxpaying public was also willing to increase support for education, at every level from kindergarten to higher education. And many affluent persons began to make sizable annual gifts to their alma maters.

In 1930 the nation spent about 3 percent of its GNP for all forms of education, public and private—elementary, secondary, and higher. By 1960 the figure stood at 5 percent and by 1970 at 7.3 percent, a striking increase within a single decade. Outlays peaked at 7.6 percent in 1975 and declined to 6.9 percent by 1980. In current dollars, public outlays amounted to just under $20 billion in 1960 and to almost $146 billion in 1981.

Between 1960 and 1980, the annual per pupil expenditure in elementary and secondary public education increased from $1,250 to $2,500 in real, noninflated dollars. Institutions of higher learning, which during this period had to accommodate a large increase in the number of students (from 3.8 to 11.6 million), raised their expenditures from $7 billion to $65 billion in current dollars, from $7 billion to $21 billion in noninflated dollars.

During the postwar decades, the annual number of college graduates increased from 288,000 in 1955 to 1,100,000 in 1980. The increase in master's degrees awarded was even more striking, from 58,000 in 1955 to 229,000 in 1980. The numbers who earned doctorates increased from 8,800 to 32,100 during these years. A total of 352,000 earned degrees were conferred in 1955; a quarter century later the total was 1.3 million. These figures provide further evidence of the magnitude of the nation's post–World War II investments to raise the educational achievement of the new generation.

Scientific and Professional Personnel

If we look at enrollments by major field of study during this period of great expansion in higher education (mid-1960s to late 1970s), we see some further interesting developments. There was

The Changing Human Resources Pool

a sizable increase in the proportion of students majoring in business. There was a steep decline in those preparing for teaching careers; some decline in those selecting social sciences as a major; and a modest increase in the proportion of students in biology and the health sciences. Finally, there were significant declines in the proportion of students in engineering, mathematics, and physical sciences—from 16.7 to 9.1 percent of the total.

Even a casual knowledge of trends in the labor market suggests that the recent generation of students was alert to changes already under way or imminent. Increasing enrollments in business were surely related to the growing demand for graduates with training in business and related fields such as accounting. The steep decline in enrollments in teacher-training courses reflected a decline in the number of young persons who wanted or who would find opportunities to work in the educational system. The upward tilt in biology and health services was linked to the continuing growth in health care employment and also to the expansion in biogenetics and related fields.

The sharp decline in the proportion of students enrolled in engineering, mathematics, and sciences, however, appears puzzling and has awakened concern. If college and postgraduate students keep close tabs on the marketplace in making their decisions about their fields of concentration, it seems hard to explain this particular trend. The recent market for engineers, mathematicians, and scientists seems to reveal strength, not weakness, and appears to stand ready to absorb additional large numbers of electrical engineers, computer specialists, mathematicians, and other scientists. However, the shortage may indicate that in a dynamic economy there are always some positions in the most rapidly growing areas that are difficult to fill, although the shortfall in the number of current graduates is usually corrected within a few years.

Does the explanation lie, perhaps, in the educational system? If students do not take the prerequisite courses in high school, either because such courses are not available or the students don't want to work hard, the pool of college students prepared to study mathematics and science will be greatly diminished. And as the nation's colleges dip lower in the pool of eligibles to fill their classes, we might expect to find a declining percentage of students prepared for and able to deal with abstract subjects.

Another line of explanation points to the hostility among young people toward science, stemming first from the youth rebellion accompanying the Vietnam War and then from the growing fear of a nuclear holocaust. There is probably a kernel of truth in each of these explanations for the declining interest among college students in science and engineering. But before we conclude that such a decline constitutes a national danger, it would be well to examine a few figures.

Between 1972 and 1981, the number of engineers employed increased from 1.1 million to 1.5 million, or by almost 40 percent; and electrical and electronic engineers, presumably among the most scarce, increased from 289,000 to 380,000, or by about one-third. Life and physical scientists increased from 232,000 to 311,000, or by approximately one-third. Engineering and science technicians had a comparable rate of increase, from 835,000 to 1.1 million.

If we look specifically at scientists and engineers employed at the cutting edge, in research and development, we again find an increase. In 1961 there was a grand total, in all sectors, of 425,000 such professionals. This figure had risen to 547,000 by 1970 and to 698,000 by 1982, a gain of approximately two-thirds over the twenty-one years.

In view of the foregoing we can probably reconcile the apparent contradiction between the declining proportion of college students in engineering and science and the increasing shift of the economy toward science-based industry. Although the relative proportion of students in these areas declined, their absolute numbers were by and large sufficient to meet the requirements of the labor market.

The Changing Human Resources Pool

This optimistic assessment finds support from a long-term comparative perspective. Until Hitler came to power, young Americans bent on careers in physics or biomedical research generally undertook a period of extended study in Europe, often in Germany. Between the start of this century and 1930, the United States won only 6 out of a total of 93 Nobel Prizes in chemistry, physics, and physiology/medicine. Each of the major West European countries—the United Kingdom, France, and Germany—accounted for between two and a half and five times as many prizes as were won by Americans. This was despite the fact that our population was considerably larger, and a much higher proportion of our youth were graduating from colleges and universities. But the post–World War II record tilts heavily in favor of the United States, even after allowance is made for Nobel Laureates who received their prizes after emigrating to this country. Out of 208 such prizes awarded between 1946 and 1981, the United States captured 109, or more than half.

We conclude, then, that the large U.S. corporations significantly increased their reliance on science and engineering personnel during the post–World War II period. They also altered their human resources policies in several other fundamental ways. First, they took advantage of the vast increase in the number of college graduates, many of whom they hired to fill their expanding line and staff positions. Second, they competed aggressively for the initially small but later growing numbers of MBAs, particularly for the graduates of the prestigious two-year schools such as Harvard, MIT, Columbia, Wharton, Carnegie-Mellon, Chicago, and Stanford. Third, they provided opportunities for "executive development" for many of their middle and higher managers whom they judged to be promotable. They paid tuition and living expenses for those who enrolled in externally sponsored courses or degree programs. In addition, an increasing number of corporations introduced and/or expanded a variety of in-house courses, usually taught by a combination of outsiders and their own specialists and senior managers.

The evidence for the trend toward hiring MBAs is quite unambiguous: the number of master's degrees conferred in business administration, commerce, and accounting rose from 4,335 in 1950 to only 4,650 in 1960 but then to 44,300 by 1980.

Although both the federal government and the private sector have made efforts to estimate the annual investment that American business makes in training its work force at all levels (from initial orientation and safety instruction to seminars for top management), the statistical base remains shaky. Under a broad definition of training, however, total annual dollar outlays run in the tens of billions. It is generally agreed that whatever the present total is, the scale of such expenditures has increased substantially. (For example, the elaborate Asbury Park yearlong residential course in the "liberal arts" that the Bell System sponsored for a decade or so for its middle managers represented the single largest corporate training commitment.) A 1981 tabulation (*Statistical Abstract of the United States, 1982–83,* p. 170) reveals that during the course of that year over 21 million persons (17 years of age or over) participated in adult education within or outside the formal educational system—about 3 out of 5 within the formal system, 2 outside. Of this total, employer-provided courses accounted for over 5 million persons and business- and industry-sponsored training for about another 3 million persons.

Corporate human resources policies have also been affected by the striking transformations in the student body in higher education during the sustained postwar boom. Most striking of all has been the increasing proportion of women students in higher education, both as undergraduate and graduate students. As late as 1960 women accounted for only slightly more than one-third of all college enrollment. In the ten-year period of 1968–1978, during which total college enrollment increased by around 20 percent, the number of female students increased from 287,000 to 601,000, or by about 110 percent—five and a half times faster than total enrollment. By 1980 there were more

The Changing Human Resources Pool

women than men college students. Other major gains in college attendance were made by blacks, and, to a somewhat lesser degree, by Asian Americans, Spanish-surnamed Americans, and native Americans. By the end of the 1970s minorities accounted for one out of every six college students.

Another important change was the narrowing of the gap between the numbers of men and women who earned advanced degrees. In 1955, 39,000 master's degrees were awarded to males, 19,000 to females. By 1980 the two received approximately the same number of degrees, about 150,000 each. As for doctorates, in 1955 men outranked women by a factor of ten: 8,000 versus 800. By 1980 the gap had narrowed appreciably, to approximately two and a half to one. The number of men who earned doctorates was 23,100; the number of women, 9,700.

This change has included a substantial rise in the proportion of women students and recent graduates in such fields as medicine, law, business (MBAs), the physical sciences, and even engineering. At the end of the 1960s, women accounted for only about 1 out of every 10 medical students; today they are at the 30 percent mark. In 1955, women accounted for 288 of the more than 8,200 recipients of law degrees, or roughly 3½ percent. In 1980, about 10,800 women were awarded law degrees out of a total of 35,700, or over 30 percent. Harvard Business School did not open its doors to women until 1959. Today in the elite business schools women account for at least one-third of the student body. In 1955, over 45,600 degrees in engineering were awarded, but only 171 of these went to women. By contrast, in 1980, women received over 7,660 of the 87,000 degrees awarded. Today women comprise about 15 percent of the freshman classes in engineering schools.

Across the board, then, the gains in higher education have been striking. In large part, they were made possible by changes that occurred in the financing of higher education. The first major shift was the G.I. Bill, passed in 1944, which enabled veterans, many of them from lower-income families, to enroll in college. In the succeeding decades the establishment of junior and community colleges, as well as branches of state universities in urban centers, greatly expanded the educational opportunities of young people from low-income families. The National Defense Education Act of 1958, following the U.S.S.R.'s first success in space, further lowered many financial barriers that had blocked many students in low-income families from pursuing higher education. The Great Society programs in the mid-1960s, which vastly expanded federal funding for student grants, loans, and work-study opportunities, to a large extent completed the task. Students from affluent families still have a substantial advantage in getting into the college of their choice. But since the mid-1960s, almost all qualified young people can gain admission to college, irrespective of the income level of their families.

Industrial and Occupational Changes

As we have seen, there is a two-way relationship between changes in the human resources pool and changes in the economy: as changes in the economy influenced the composition of the labor force, so the better educated and trained work force contributed to altering the industrial and occupational profile. A good place to begin a review of these transformations is with agriculture. In 1930, one out of approximately every five Americans was still gainfully occupied in farming. Of the 10 million persons so employed, about 6 million were farm owners or managers and the remainder were foremen or laborers. The comparable figures for 1980 are 1.5 million owners or managers and another 1.2 million foremen or laborers. Overall, farmers accounted for less than 3 percent of the working population, down from 20 percent in 1930. This striking shrinkage came about as a result of major changes in technology, in the national and international economy, and in the human resources pool.

The Changing Human Resources Pool

Farms became much larger and capital investments soared. The illiterate sharecropper was replaced by an owner/manager who had acquired a bachelor's or master's degree, relied on airplane spraying to control pests, used a computer to guide his planning and sales, and sought the help of a tax accountant before making his investment decisions. The radical changes in farming were directly linked to complementary changes in the skills and competence of farm owners and managers.

Table 5.1 sets forth the shifts over the past 50 years in the percentage distribution of employment in the nonagricultural sectors of the economy. The outstanding changes are substantial shrinkage in mining, manufacturing, and transportation, with equivalent gains in services and government. During these decades, in other words, the U.S. economy shifted away from a focus on the production of goods to a focus on the production of services. Today services account for about 70 percent of all income and employment.

TABLE 5.1
Percentage Distribution of Nonagricultural Employment by Major Industry Division, 1930, 1950, 1960, and 1980

Industry Division	1930	1950	1960	1980
Mining	3.4	2.0	1.3	1.1
Contract construction	4.7	5.2	5.4	4.9
Manufacturing	32.3	33.5	31.0	22.4
Transportation and utilities	12.6	8.9	7.4	5.7
Wholesale and retail trade	20.8	21.6	21.0	22.5
Finance, insurance, real estate	4.8	4.1	4.9	5.7
Services	10.6	11.3	13.6	19.8
Government	10.8	13.5	15.4	17.9

SOURCE: Data compiled from U.S. Department of Commerce, *The Statistical Abstract of the United States.*

Table 5.2 sets out the major shifts in the occupational groupings of American workers. We can observe that in addition to the substantial shrinkage in the number of farm workers noted earlier, there has been a relative shrinkage among blue-collar workers, with more than proportionate increases among the white-collar workers. Within the white-collar group, the largest gains occurred among those with the highest qualifications, that is, among professional and technical workers. The table obscures a further significant shift within the category of managers and administrators. In the earlier period, this category included many small businessmen; in the later period, it included a much larger number of staff and line personnel in corporations, government agencies, and large nonprofit institutions. In 1960, the proportion of salaried versus self-employed managers was approximately

TABLE 5.2

Percentage Distribution of Employed Workers by Major Occupational Group, 1930, 1950, 1960, and 1980*

Occupation	1930	1950	1960	1980
White collar	29.4	37.5	43.4	52.2
Professional and technical	6.8	7.5	11.4	16.1
Managers and administrators	7.4	10.8	10.7	11.2
Salesworkers	6.3	6.4	6.4	6.3
Clerical	8.9	12.8	14.8	18.6
Blue collar	39.6	39.1	36.6	31.7
Craftsmen and kindred workers	12.8	12.9	13.0	12.9
Operatives	15.8	20.4	18.2	14.2
Nonfarm laborers	9.8	5.9	5.4	4.6
Service workers	9.8	11.0	12.2	13.3
Farm workers, including managers	21.2	12.4	7.9	2.8

* The 1930 figures are for economically active workers.
SOURCE: Data compiled from U.S. Department of Commerce, *The Statistical Abstract of the United States.*

The Changing Human Resources Pool

equal; by 1980, the ratio had shifted to about 5 to 1 in favor of the salaried manager. A final striking change, evident from the table, is the increase in the proportion of clerical workers. In 1980 they comprised the single largest group, even though they had been one of the smallest groups fifty years earlier.

We are now in a better position to trace the ways in which the changing pool of human resources has affected and been affected by the transformations that have occurred in the U.S. economy.

The postwar period, especially since 1960, has seen several new sources of entrants into the labor force. The main new sources have been married women, members of the baby boom generation, and immigrants. A fourth source has been the many hitherto underutilized members of farm families, primarily in the South, who relocated to urban centers in search of regular employment. About nine out of ten members of this enlarged labor force found employment in the service sector of the economy, that is, outside of agriculture, mining, manufacturing, and construction; they found jobs primarily in retailing, finance, and banking, government, and services (narrowly defined). Many of the married women sought and found part-time employment in retailing.

During the postwar period the median level of educational preparation increased substantially; newcomers to the labor force had acquired on average about one year of postsecondary education. There is no question that the tilting of the economy toward services, with clerical occupations undergoing the most rapid expansion, served to spur prospective workers to obtain more schooling. The increasing sophistication of the goods-producing sector, as noted in the earlier discussion of agriculture, also encouraged more young people to stay in school long enough to acquire additional competences.

Even in such unsophisticated jobs as domestic worker, taxicab operator, waiter, all at the lower end of the service hierarchy, workers need skills that will enable them, for example, to communicate clearly by radio or phone, write down messages, keep records of trips, and use tables to calculate taxes. And although graduation from high school may not be necessary for entrance into these jobs, it is usually a prerequisite for any supervisory position.

The growth of services also facilitated the absorption of large numbers of immigrants, legal and illegal. Consider the success of the many Asians in retailing; the large numbers of students from abroad who drive taxicabs; the extent to which newcomers from Central and South America have helped to staff nursing homes; or the role of the Chinese as restaurateurs. Many immigrants have also found their way into lower-paying jobs in agriculture, manufacturing, and construction, jobs that in certain labor-market areas have failed to attract adequate numbers of native-born Americans.

Let us now shift our focus to the upper end of the educational-occupational hierarchy—to the relationships between the explosive growth of the college-trained population, and the transformations in industrial and occupational structures. Here we find, first, that the growth of government led to an enlarged demand for college-trained persons to fill a wide range of positions. For example, teachers were needed to staff the burgeoning school systems, as were engineers to plan and build the national highway network, and scientists trained in a variety of disciplines to oversee the government's large R&D efforts in biomedical research and space and defense programs. Moreover, the armed services moved to staff their officer corps almost exclusively with college graduates. The rising incomes of the American public during the postwar era also spurred the expansion of the numbers of independent professionals such as physicians, lawyers, dentists, architects, accountants, psychologists, and many others, most of whom can qualify for practice only after an extended period of higher education. However, the largest employer of the vastly expanded numbers of college and postgraduate students is the corporation.

The Large Corporation and the Changing
Human Resources Pool

The proliferation of large organizations in every sector—private, nonprofit, and government—created a strong demand for managers and administrators, most of whom were recruited from among college or professional school graduates. This trend fit with employer needs; that is, employers decided that the planning, operating, and control functions on which their complex organizations depended could best be handled by individuals with specialized training in quantitative methods and analytical procedures, and with adequate levels of skill in oral and written communications.

Another factor contributing to the growing need for specialists—particularly those skilled in the law, accounting, finance, economics, marketing, and communications—was the internationalization of the U.S. economy. Still another factor was the increasing complexity of relationship between the private and public sectors, itself a consequence of large-scale increases in federal spending and the expanded role of government as regulator.

There is always an accommodation between changes in the economy and changes in the human resources pool, although temporary discrepancies in the demand and supply for particular groups of workers are inevitable in an economy characterized by change. During the past half century, the large corporation has played a leading role in this process of accommodation. The steeply rising demand of large corporations for college and graduate degree recipients, underwritten by good initial job offers and attractive career prospects, encouraged millions of young Americans to stay on the educational track until their mid-twenties or later. They were willing to forego immediate job opportunities, even accept financial help from their parents, or work for some of their expenses, in order to obtain the college or higher degree that was their card of entry into the world of the corporate manager.

For the most part those who had grown up during the Depression and World War II looked with favor on corporate employment, which offered them a good starting salary, good fringe benefits, and lifelong security. The unsettled environment of their childhood years had scarred their parents and themselves, and they found it relatively easy to adjust to the negative aspects and the routines that characterized most large enterprises.

In contrast, those who completed their schooling after the middle or late 1960s had grown up in a more supportive environment: Economic growth, expanding employment opportunities, and substantial gains in real income appeared to be here to stay. Accordingly, these young people had both more career options and higher expectations than their parents. They were less willing to settle for a job that merely paid well and offered a reasonably secure future. They wanted meaningful jobs and careers that offered opportunities for self-fulfillment and allowed them to pursue a life-style of their own choosing.

But most large companies, facing a more slowly growing economy and eroding markets, were in no position to meet these expanded expectations. With the bloom off the economy, many of the new entrants adjusted their expectations downward to bring them more into congruence with the new reality. But this lowering of expectations did not come without cost to both the individual and to the corporate employer. Many of the young managers were disappointed with their work environments, and their performance was adversely affected by their unmet expectations.

Some large corporations have gradually become aware that they confront new challenges and have begun to explore different ways of responding to their trainees. Others, however, oblivious to what has been going on, have continued to rely on their

The Changing Human Resources Pool

established human resources policies and practices, which have only added to the underlying tension.

The growing confrontation can be summarized in terms of the pressures being exerted by today's better-prepared young people who want meaningful work and challenging career opportunities and the difficulties that the large corporation has in adjusting its organizational structures and human resources policies to respond to these new expectations.

PART III

Scale and Managers

6

Scale, Structure, and Decision Making

In all fairness, we must acknowledge a simple fact. Many large corporations have been in the black for a long time, and most of them are likely to remain profitable for many years to come. This having been said we can look at the other side of the picture. Many large corporations, including those with good records of growth and profits, are increasingly confronted with inefficiencies in their decision-making mechanisms and in their human resources policies. These inefficiencies are directly linked to the ways in which they have responded to the challenges of scale. The continuing difficulties that many "smokestack" industries are experiencing, the uncertain future of the automobile industry, and the bail-out of Continental Illinois are a few examples of the serious problems that many large corporations confront.

An increasing number of our leading corporate firms have entered into or are now contemplating some type of joint venture with the Japanese. Not one of these developments, much less all of them, would have been given credence as recently as five years ago, even in a futuristic planning exercise. Clearly, many large corporations face major challenges despite and, as we shall see, because of their scale.

Among economists there are two schools of thought about the changing role of the large corporation in the U.S. economy. One school holds that on the basis of data relating to market shares, financial assets, and employment, the large corporation has been growing at the expense of small and medium-sized firms. In support of this interpretation they point to the fact in many industries the three or four largest firms account for an increasing proportion of total activity. As these analysts read the evidence, the growing proportion of the economy controlled by large firms reflects their superior ability to exploit the advantages of scale.

The second school concurs with the finding that the large corporation is dominant in many sectors of the economy, especially in manufacturing, public utilities and communications, department stores, financial institutions, and many new service sectors (such as hotel, fast food, and car rental chains). At the same time, these economists question the growing dominance of the large firm. They note that industries and firms are characterized by a life cycle and that at some point growth and profits are likely to level off and then decline. Moreover, they are skeptical about the hypothesis that a large corporation in a mature industry which pursues an active divestiture-acquisition policy will be able to achieve for a second or a third time the rate of growth that it enjoyed initially.

Our concern is not to weigh the merits of these contrasting views. From a long-term vantage, it appears that the truth may lie somewhere between: large corporations now account for a greater proportion of the total output than in earlier generations, but considerable opportunity remains for the emergence of new profitable firms and for the continuing prosperity of many medium-sized firms.

Scale, Structure, and Decision Making

The Structural and Decision-Making Changes
Accompanying Growth

As we begin to explore the dimensions of scale, our first task is to examine more closely the modifications in the structure and decision-making processes that accompany the transformation of a small firm into a large corporation. A single individual or, sometimes, a small group of associates plays the critical role in the management of the small firm as it finds its niche in the market on the basis of a new product or process. The owner-managers must be willing to risk all their capital and to invest all their time and energy in the new venture if they want to see increased output lead to increased sales and increased profits. When the profits are reinvested (and often augmented by additional funds from outside the company), the result may be a repetition of the growth cycle, again and again. It is the cumulative effects of these repeated cycles that transform the small enterprise into a medium-sized or, occasionally, a large corporation. Wang and Tandem, among others, are recent examples of this transformation.

Whether the benign cycle gets started and how long it continues depends very much on the external environment. The long post–World War II boom created a highly supportive environment, which helped many small U.S. corporations make it into the big leagues.

We can gain a first view of the impact of scale on structure by considering the typical management of a small or medium-sized firm. The owner or owners are directly involved in almost all aspects of the firm's operations and consult frequently and informally on important issues. More often than not, all of the firm's activities are carried on in a single location. This, of course, facilitates informal interchanges. The decision-making horizons are relatively short, and planning usually extends no further than a forecast of the next quarter's or next year's sales. While there is some specialization among the owner-managers, all top executives are generally involved in key decisions.

In order to exploit the opportunities that the market presents, salesmen are hired to devote most or all of their time to increasing the number of active customers. In a manufacturing company that is undergoing rapid growth, one or more managers will concentrate on operating the plant. As manufacturing expands, the procurement function may be split off and one or more persons assigned to purchasing. By this time, the firm is continually hiring employees in a wide range of areas—in sales, manufacturing, procurement, warehousing functions, and such support services as accounting and finance. Since the buildup of the work force can no longer be left to the earlier informal procedures, where senior executives identified and hired the new employees, a personnel department is usually established.

In the normal course of growth, a functionalized system of management evolves, in which a number of subsidiary managers oversee and control major functions in order to reduce the burden on those at the top. But at some point, the very success of the functionalized approach leads to new strains. The chief executive and his key associates often find themselves still caught up in the details of daily operations. At the same time, the subsidiary managers generally want more freedom to act on their own.

Under these circumstances, the senior officials are likely to initiate another set of structural changes, leading to the establishment of a divisionalized structure, in which the heads of the new divisions are given considerable scope to run their operations as long as they meet their budgets and other goals. Whereas the earlier informal and then functionalized pattern may have led to considerable jockeying for position and power among members of the management team, the process is likely to accelerate once divisions are established and managers are given more authority and responsibility.

Scale, Structure, and Decision Making

The Development of an Internal Reporting System

The chief executives of a growing company are often at a different location from the managers responsible for divisionalized activities and, consequently, cannot continue to interact with them on an informal basis. An internal reporting system must therefore be established so that those at the top can keep abreast of the performance of the operating units. As the divisions proliferate, these reports tend to become more elaborate. And as more data are produced and flow upward, and questions for clarification and elaboration flow downward, there is an increasing need for staff personnel whose primary or sole responsibility is the preparation, analysis, and/or follow-up of these elaborate reporting systems. Frequently, critical data that a CEO needs in order to make important decisions do not find their way to his desk, or do so only after long delay, while irrelevant information clogs the channels. For example, one CEO recently visited a consultant carrying a 500-page computer printout detailing the performance of his company's 250 profit centers. Despite this plethora of data, the company had stalled for three years before deciding on a necessary divestiture. Too much information can inhibit action just as too little information can lead to a poor decision.

In a large corporation a reporting system must do more than provide up-to-date figures that reflect the performance of each operating division. Top management needs forecasts of the next year's (and subsequent) levels of activity, the divisions' requirements for new capital, and other critical information bearing on future sales, revenues, and profits. Hence most large corporations institute planning and budgeting cycles that generate flows of paper, discussions, arguments, and appraisals and lead finally to decisions about goals and resources allocations.

In some large companies, the annual planning exercise commands considerable time and effort, because when the figures that the units send to the top are accepted, they become their targets for the next year. As long as the economy is free of large-scale fluctuations, these planning and budgeting exercises are highly useful in a decentralized corporation; in fact, they are essential. But whenever the market takes an unexpected turn—either up or down—these exercises can provide only limited guidance. And, recently, radical shifts in the business climate have become increasingly frequent.

Many managements have responded by asking for a review of forecasts on a semiannual, quarterly, or even monthly basis. Such a response is especially likely if shifts in the economy are accompanied by a sharp drop in sales, a large buildup in inventories, or other unpleasant and unexpected developments. When those at the top become uneasy, operating officials are asked to prepare additional reports. In some corporations, report writing seems to take on a life of its own and often deflects attention and energy from profit-making decisions. Senior managers of foreign subsidiaries often complain about this issue of report writing, saying that it makes them in essence high-class clerks, not country managers.

Internal corporate reporting and analyses provide the basis for more than operating and strategic decisions by top management and its subordinate managers. Current operating results and future estimates of sales and profits are released to stockholders. In public companies, these reports attract the scrutiny of security analysts, providing them with important data for their recommendations to buy and sell. Since senior executives often own significant amounts of stock in their companies and have stock options, they have a personal stake in the evaluations that the stock market places on their company's shares. If the company is considering raising additional capital through a new issue of stock, the assessment of the stock market becomes even more important. One of the tasks of a CEO in a young, growing company is to make the rounds of the security analysts and inform them, through group and individual presentations, about his company and the outlook for its future growth. Even if the company is not planning to raise additional capital in the near future, reports by security analysts recommending the stock for purchase can result in significant gains for those who hold shares. Moreover, the increased visibility of the company speaks to easier access to the market in the future.

It is a chore for the analysts to appraise small companies on a fast track because they have not had time to be fully tested or to reveal how well they are managed and how reliable their reporting is. Even large, established companies find it difficult to persuade security analysts that their next quarter's sales and profits will reach a designated level since time often reveals that their estimates were wide of the mark.

On April 23, 1984, the *Wall Street Journal* carried a column on a suit by a holder of U.S. Surgical stock against the firm's directors over alleged overstatement of earnings. The Securities and Exchange Commission (SEC) had earlier charged the firm with overstating its pretax earnings by at least $18.4 million from 1979 through 1981. The defendants consented to a court order barring them from future violations without admitting or denying the charges.

The oversight of the SEC, the professionalism of public acountants, and the sophistication of the security analysts all help to assure that corporate reporting conforms to prevailing practices. Deliberate falsification of reports in large enterprises is rare. During the recent years of inflation, however, accountants have found it difficult to agree on the adjustments required for appropriate reporting of profits and valuation of assets.

The complexity of measuring corporate performance in an inflationary period is underlined by the following quote from *Business Week*'s (March 21, 1984) "Corporate Scoreboard": "Sales and dividends for the nation's 500 largest industrial corporations rose, on average, 10% a year or better during the past five years. That's what the financial statements based on traditional historical-cost accounting indicate. But when the results are adjusted for the ravages of inflation, sales and dividends showed virtually no growth . . . after-tax profits under historical-cost measurements rose 6% annually. Under inflation-adjusted acccounting, however, corporate earnings posted a 2% annual decline."

The 1983 *Annual Report* of Exxon further demonstrates the distortions introduced by inflation. Earnings per share for 1981, 1982, and 1983 are reported as $5.58, $4.82, and $7.78 respectively. But when the inflation adjustment has been made, the earnings per share for these three years turn out to be $1.92, a loss of 35 cents, and $1.89. The combined totals for the three years in current dollars amounted to $18.18 versus $3.46 in real dollars. Even more striking is the added comment in the balance sheet: "In other words it would take $64 billion [1983 dollars] to provide the same purchasing power as the $29 billion represented in the financial statements."

An inflationary environment also adds to the difficulties that senior management faces in steering a large corporation and taking actions to assure its future. *Fortune*'s ten-year review (April 30, 1984) of the 500 largest U.S. industrial companies showed a combined net profit of $68.8 billion for 1983, excluding the losses suffered by the 60 unprofitable corporations. If the reduced value of the dollar as a result of inflation is taken into account, this sum was 20 percent less than the $43.6 billion that they had earned in 1974. These modest earnings are even more striking when we remember that over the decade these companies invested and reinvested more than $300 billion in their businesses.

The difficulties that inflation causes for the valuation of assets are especially great in the case of fixed plant and equipment. And when assets take the form of investments in countries whose currency is undergoing wide gyrations in relation to the dollar, valuation is further complicated. Large corporations are likely to face both of these circumstances.

Scale, Structure, and Decision Making

Alternative Growth Strategies

Fortune's 1984 report presented several additional interesting findings. First, the most successful companies during the bleak decade that saw the Dow drop by 33 percent in inflation-adjusted terms did not come out ahead by borrowing heavily at the early stages of the inflation and then paying off their debts with cheap dollars at the end of the period. Rather, their success was grounded in concentrating their activities in the markets they knew, maintaining product leadership, and keeping tight controls on their costs.

A second interesting finding relates to the alternative strategies these companies confronted in deciding what to do with their earnings. Several paid out between 50 and 70 percent to the stockholders. Some recently began to repurchase their own stock, believing this to be one of the soundest ways to improve returns for their stockholders. And others moved cautiously when it came to acquiring other companies.

To drive home the last lesson, the *Fortune* report looked at seven large mergers during that decade which had left the acquiring companies in worse shape. These included Mobil Oil with Marcor, Sohio with Kennicott, Exxon with Reliance Electric, and Atlantic Richfield with Anaconda. The 1983 earnings of these acquiring companies would have been on the average between 20 and 40 percent higher had they not entered into the merger.

It is not surprising, however, that these highly successful large companies as well as many other smaller ones have aggressively pursued an acquisition route as the preferred way to use the large profits that they earned from their special niche in the market. Since antitrust legislation frequently prevents horizontal mergers, these companies are able to maintain their rate of growth and profits only through the acquisition route. And, of course, most managements favor continued growth for a variety of reinforcing reasons.

First, a growing corporation attracts individuals with talent. Able managers seek more responsibility, more authority, and greater financial rewards, and a growing company is best able to meet these demands. Growth also makes it easier for a corporation to tolerate heavy overhead, excessive costs, and redundant personnel. Senior executives enjoy leading a large company, and their compensation is usually geared to sales and profits. Stockholders and the stock market also respond favorably to strong growth.

But there are some important negatives frequently associated with growth based on acquisitions. The acquiring company may pay too high a premium and/or may not have the specialized knowledge to judge correctly changes in the market that may lie just beyond the horizon. Surely both of these factors played a role in the unsuccessful mergers reviewed by *Fortune*. A more subtle difficulty, alluded to earlier, is the strain that the acquisition places on scarce managerial resources. The acquiring company's management may not be able to find one or more key executives in its own ranks to oversee the newly acquired enterprise. And if the absorption does not work out smoothly, as is frequently the case, the time and effort of senior management can be spread too thin. This helps to explain why many large corporations have recently decided to divest themselves of the divisions that are not integral to their business. They feel that on balance they have more to gain by focusing on what they know best.

Another consequence of the slowed growth—in many cases the no-growth—that characterized many large corporations during the recent recession was that they had to pay attention to the uncontrolled expansion that had earlier taken place in their management ranks. As the automotive, steel, farm machinery, and other leading sectors of U.S. industry ran into hard times after 1979, they found it necessary and possible to slash their

Scale, Structure, and Decision Making

management ranks not by a few hundred but by many thousands. Another *Fortune* survey (February 6, 1984) declared that more than half of all corporations, and between 75 and 90 percent of those experiencing no growth or intense foreign competition, reduced their rolls of middle managers between August 1982 and August 1983. The article noted that Xerox reduced its headquarters staff in Stamford, Connecticut, by one-third and that Illinois Bell reduced the number of its managers earning between $50,000 and $100,000 from 3,000 to 1,900. The new American business slogan is lean and mean.

The managements of successful corporations are not only likely to be tripped up by the onset and persistence of a recession; they can trip themselves up even when the economy and their industry are upbeat. Let's look briefly at two possible sources of difficulties: making investment decisions and managing the R&D function.

The evidence suggests that the large U.S. steel companies owe their current difficulties to, among other factors, their policy of distributing capital investments over many plants, rather than concentrating to gain technological leadership in a few plants with state of the art technologies. The minimills, in contrast to the large integrated companies, pursued a more focused policy with outstanding success. Over the past two decades they pushed their market share from 2.5 percent to 20 percent, and it is possible that by the end of the century they will account for half of the U.S. domestic steel output (*New York Times,* February 24, 1984). The owner of a Texas minimill who exchanges detailed cost data with a Japanese counterpart has found that the two mills are producing in the same cost range. It is the large integrated companies that are noncompetitive, not the entire industry.

Increasing attention has been focused in recent years on the importance of innovation as the basis for maintaining corporate and national leadership. But relatively little attention has been paid to the difficulties that most large science-based corporations face in managing their R&D operations. Over the years even the leading industrial companies such as General Electric, DuPont, and Westinghouse have encountered difficulty in achieving what they had hoped for from their investments in R&D. After some initial years of effort, GE considered it the better part of wisdom to withdraw from advanced work in nuclear energy. And some years later it turned its back on computers. What accounts for the difficulties in managing the R&D function?

It is conventional wisdom at DuPont that Wallace Caruthers, who in the late 1930s developed nylon and thus laid the foundation for the synthetic fiber industry, would not have been able to cope with the paperwork and financial controls that governed the laboratory in the postwar period when each research proposal on its way up for funding and down for implementation had to be initialed by seven managers. But there is no single explanation for the continuing difficulties on the R&D front nor shall we make a blanket indictment of the total effort. Many of the leading technological achievements of the last decades— from television to the moon shot—were achieved by large U.S. companies.

Vladimir Zworykin, a major contributor to the development of television, felt that his many contributions would have been impossible without the faith and confidence of David Sarnoff, RCA's CEO, in his ability to invent. Charlotte Chandler (*The Ultimate Seduction*, 1984) quotes Zworykin: "Sarnoff would say to me, 'How much will you need?' I always said forty thousand dollars. I never knew the price. He had perfect faith in me. The only question he ever asked after that was 'What's it going to do?' " (p. 158) But this preferred working relationship is often not attainable. Most senior executives are uneasy when they see the continuing large flows of dollars into research and nothing emerging at the other end. The gap between research administrators and bench scientists, particularly in fields undergoing rapid change, is a continual source of tension. Those in control of the purse strings frequently have only limited knowledge with which to judge the proposals before them.

When we look at two of the most flourishing areas of U.S. technology—computers and biotechnology—we are impressed with the significant leadership role of university based or affiliated scientists-technologists. We can identify several gains for R&D from this constellation: a dominant role for researchers in their twenties and thirties; the absence of extended lines of authority required to obtain approval for projects; and payments in the form of stock for those who contribute to significant break-throughs.

Nevertheless, the difficulties of managing R&D in a corporate environment should not be minimized. The outstanding success story has been Bell Labs, a success predicated on AT&T's protected position, which enabled the company to set aside large sums and adhere to distant goals without worrying about the effect of investments in research on its balance sheet. The recent *Fortune* story (September 5, 1983) on Xerox's carefully nurtured Palo Alto research laboratory, PARC, suggests that in the more dynamic environment of office machines, computers, and communications, even tender loving care may not suffice. The article suggested that the linkages between Palo Alto and Rochester, New York, were so fragile that the advances in the laboratory were seldom transmitted into improved and new products, at least not by Xerox.

Schlumberger's outstanding success over many decades has unquestionably been grounded in a long-term policy of investment in R&D. An interest in science and technology was the driving force that motivated one of the founding members, and it has remained the primary commitment of its current highly successful chief executive, Jean Riboud (Ken Auletta, *The Art of Corporate Success,* 1984).

Thus R&D, as a critical engine for continued growth and leadership, confronts the management of our largest enterprises with a major challenge, the answers to which remain elusive. It may turn out that there is a permanent nonfit between the conditions required for the leadership of a strong R&D operation and the imperatives of large corporate enterprises. We may have to look primarily to smaller companies for most of the innovative breakthroughs. The large corporations may be best at adapting the new technology to the mass market.

Norman McCrae, the deputy editor of *The Economist,* first warned about the coming decline of the corporate giants in the mid-1970s. He recently returned to the theme, "Entrepreneurial Now—Big Goes Bust" (April 17, 1982), stressing his view that organizational size had reached a point where managers and workers could no longer perform effectively. The one promising development that he saw was the recent effort by IBM and other well-run corporations to experiment with in-house quasi-entrepreneurial divisions freed from the heavy weight of bureaucratic oversight and control. How far or fast their innovation takes hold, however, remains to be seen. A senior IBM executive noted a recent situation in which the corporate planners asked for representatives from such an entrepreneurial unit at one of its meetings and were told that nobody would show up since the agenda was not relevant to the division's concerns!

To summarize, as a small company becomes transformed into a successful large corporation by exploiting its special niche in the marketplace, it accumulates a cushion that can continue to speed its growth. If the company wants to maintain a high growth rate, it will usually have to acquire other companies. The acquisition process itself, however, is fraught with dangers and difficulties, none greater than the demands it makes on a limited pool of scarce managerial talent. The principal alternative for maintaining a high rate of growth and leadership is a strong R&D function. This alternative is also difficult, however, because of the differences in the values and behavior patterns of senior executives and talented researchers and the time frames within which they are bounded.

Scale, Structure, and Decision Making

There are, then, no easy answers for the successful large corporation that seeks to maintain its momentum. And the challenges it faces become all the more evident when we focus, as we will now, on the impact of increasing scale on the decision-making process.

The Impact of Scale on Decision Making

When the corporation was small, most of the information that the key executives required became available to them as a by-product of their ongoing duties supplemented by some specific details from the accounting office. Since the key executives met many times during the day to consider pressing issues, a basic informality governed their decision making. They knew each other's strengths and weaknesses in dealing with present realities and future plans, and they could simply make the necessary allowances in order to reach a consensus. The shared objective of speeding the corporation's growth, preferably from internally generated funds, commanded the allegiance of all of the senior executives. Their acceptance of a common mission, reinforced by their common experience and common expectations, helped to create an environment in which decision making was both informal and speedy. But scale brings many changes, many not for the best.

In a large corporation with multiple divisions the decision-making process requires a formal structure: efforts must be made to invite all who have a stake in the outcome; necessary information must be prepared in advance; and those who participate must have an opportunity to speak. Since a large divisionalized corporation often has up to, and sometimes more than, five layers of management, arranging a meeting of all interested parties and running it efficiently is not easy; it may be impossible. Even the most carefully designed structure and procedures cannot assure that all who participate will say what they mean and mean what they say. Middle and senior managers have ongoing relations with their associates and subordinates, and the issues taken up at one day's conference are often linked to what was decided the day before or what is on the next day's agenda. Accordingly, each participant weighs what he has to say in terms of the degree of risk he is willing to incur, knowing that he may come out ahead if events prove him right and that he will lose standing if the decision and its consequences find him on the wrong side. The upshot is that many participants seek a safe place in the middle.

The question of who should be invited to a decision-making conference is itself often far from simple. In a large, complex organization many different divisions and executives may have at least peripheral interest in the items to be discussed and decided. Since the process of reaching a decision becomes geometrically more complex as the participants increase, there are good reasons on grounds of efficiency to keep the number small. But critical dimensions of the problem may not surface and surely will not be given their due unless those who have the relevant specialized knowledge are present.

There is a further reason for broad consultation. Since decisions, once taken, must be implemented, those likely to be significantly affected should have an opportunity to participate in the process. If they are ignored, they may be less than enthusiastic when it comes time for them to help implement the decision. They may give it only half-hearted support because they never had an opportunity to see the larger picture into which it fits.

Eliciting the participation of many individuals from different parts of the organization admittedly is not free of costs; a considerable amount of time may be required to first solicit inputs and then sift them. But the alternative of limited consultation and participation carries a much greater risk that the implementation process will founder.

In attempting to explain the high-level performance of the

Scale, Structure, and Decision Making

Japanese economy, a number of analysts have directed attention to its corporate decision-making process in which extended consultation is the prelude to achieving a consensual decision. Admittedly extended consultation is time-consuming, but the analysts stress that if one extends the time span of the decision-making process to include the implementation processes, broad consultation pays off.

In the absence of more knowledge than we currently have, it is difficult to reach a definitive judgment about the Japanese decision-making process. Many U.S. businessmen who have had extensive experience with the Japanese on their home ground believe that their process of extended prior consultation frequently prevents them from moving in time to exploit opportunities that the market presents.

We noted earlier that one of the concomitants of divisionalization is the determination of each unit to protect and, wherever possible, enhance its area of responsibility and control. Since important issues for discussion and resolution on the corporate agenda may result in a shift in the relative power and prestige of divisions, the decision-making process will often be attenuated by the defensive and offensive actions of divisions potentially affected.

Faced with the probability of disagreement, even conflict, among major divisions, a customary response of top management is to encourage the parties that have a stake in the outcome to get together and work out a mutually acceptable solution or at least to narrow the differences among them. Such an approach has much to commend it. If difficulties can be resolved by those directly affected, the time and energies of executives at the top can be conserved. Further, by instructing the interested parties to work the problem out, top management has issued an implicit warning that unless they do, the decision will be taken out of their hands and will almost surely result in a more drastic outcome for the losing party or parties.

There is another reason that top management prefers this

procedure, whereby agreed-upon recommendations are submitted to it for review and approval. A large organization requires that its managers and groups cooperate on a continuing basis to promote corporate goals and objectives. Sharp conflicts and defeats leave hard feelings. If they can be exorcised from the decision-making process, long-term cooperation among the several divisions will be enhanced.

But there are downside risks to having solutions worked out from below. One relates to timing; since each of the concerned units will attempt to keep its power and influence intact, each will move cautiously, even slowly. And when the problem is finally settled to the satisfaction of all, the resolution is likely to fall short of what is needed. Only those at the top have the overview and the muscle required to push through a tough decision. If they always give precedence to maintaining peace, the issues may never be resolved, only postponed.

Obstacles in Responding to Change

How, then, does a large corporation with an elongated, highly structured decision-making process respond quickly and effectively to a market that is becoming increasingly demanding and volatile? The obstacles to a quick response are, as we have seen, built into the process. The corporation has evolved an organizational structure in which specific values, rules, and routines facilitate the interactions among divisions and managers so that many responses have a semipredictable quality. The managers have learned from experience the parameters within which their responses must be developed. The longer the corporation has been following well-grooved paths with satisfactory or superior results, the more the management cadre has absorbed the basics that guide its behavior. These ingrained response mechanisms continue to guide managerial behavior even after market signals have begun to change. In fact, the initial signs that the market has begun to shift in terms of consumer preferences, prices, new competitors, and/or substitute materials are likely to be ignored or downplayed because of the ingrained behavior of managers based on their past successes.

There are also good reasons for caution and constraint when management hesitates to deviate from established policies and practices. Much of the strength of a large organization grows precisely out of the fact that its smooth-running mechanisms give people in different parts of the organization reasonably clear ideas about how to act and react. When markets are going through seasonal or cyclical gyrations, perhaps the best response is to rely once again on responses that have proved successful in the past. A decision to do something new and different, especially if it involves major changes in policy or procedures, cannot be taken lightly because of the considerable disturbances, or "costs," that such shifts are likely to bring in their wake. Therefore, there is a strong bias on the part of top management to hold a steady course as long as possible, in the hope—reinforced by experience—that the market will soon right itself.

This bias on the part of top managers is encouraged by their awareness that their cushion will allow them to tolerate considerable reductions in profits in certain divisions as long as others continue to perform well. In short, they believe they have the wherewithal to weather short-term buffeting.

And they are reinforced in their preference for continuity over change by the knowledge, experience, and know-how that they have acquired over the years—often over decades and generations—about their sector of the economy, which is now sending forth danger signals. Much of the continuing success of a large corporation is predicated on its accumulated experience in a particular sector of the economy, where it understands, better than others, the ways in which changes in raw materials, capacity, technology, demand, and prices act and interact. This special know-how and knowledge, distilled from decades of experience, has helped to guide and direct the corporation's responses to the changing market. It should be no surprise, then, that the corporation will be relatively slow to recognize, and even slower to admit, that the market in which it has long been a leader is undergoing a radical shift and may permanently shrink. The recent failure of the major steel, automobile, and rubber tire firms to correctly assess the changes in the markets where they had long been successful exemplify this problem. "Big U.S. oil companies, once fat and happy, have been eliminating jobs by the tens of thousands, and white collar employees have been the hardest hit." The opening paragraph of a *Wall Street Journal* article (April 19, 1984) encapsulated this point. Exxon eliminated 17,000 jobs in 1983—10 percent of its entire worldwide work force. "We need to get down to fighting trim."

There are additional reasons why top management is likely to move slowly to accept the evidence that the market has taken a permanent turn for the worse. In large corporations, there is considerable distance between those in middle management and those at the top, and the middle managers who first perceive the danger signals may not want or be able to share the information with those in a position to respond. Their own supervisors, one or two rungs up the ladder, may decide that they have more to gain than to lose in keeping the bad news to themselves. Hence, considerable time may pass before those at the top understand that a specific sector of their business may be entering into long-term decline.

Other organizational difficulties may also come into play. Even if the downbeat information is passed along, those at the top may conclude that no response is possible until the situation has been carefully reassessed. They establish a committee to make the assessment and to outline alternative recommendations. The committee may find its assignment not only difficult but disagreeable, especially if the preferred options include a recommendation of cutbacks or even divestments that could place the jobs and careers of committee members and others with whom they are closely aligned at risk. Rather than make such drastic recommendations, the committee will try to find a way to stall and pass the buck back up to the top. In such a case, the senior management once again has the problem on its agenda, but now considerable time has passed since the market began to weaken and the options for taking constructive action at small cost may have evaporated.

Further delay can occur if the chief executive officer is close to retirement and decides to leave the difficult decision to his successor. If the division that is in trouble is one with which he has been closely identified over the years, his temptation to procrastinate is strengthened since he does not want to leave in an atmosphere of trouble, turmoil, and tension. His associates at the top may also prefer to table the decision. As the CEO nears retirement, those competing to succeed him become increasingly cautious and circumspect. Each of the leading contenders appreciates that he has little to gain and lots to lose if he becomes an active participant in a difficult decision that will upset both his associates and the board. Most managers feel that it is better to sidestep the issue until the new CEO is appointed. When the winning contender gets the nod to lead the corporation, he can take decisive action at smaller personal risk. Again, of course, it may be too late.

There are other reasons that senior management is often excruciatingly slow to recognize, and particularly to act on its recognition, that the past is no longer prologue and that the corporation must take radical action. We earlier called attention to the fact that even after a large corporation realizes that its best move is to divest itself of a product, process, or business in which it has had a significant role, it may move slowly and deliberately in order to insure that the key people who will be separated will be satisfactorily placed. Management understands that it can face adverse repercussions if other executives come to believe that the next time they may be summarily discharged.

The delay may have little to do, however, with management's

concern for the personnel that will soon be discharged. Often it reflects the difficulty of locating a buyer for a division. At certain times potential buyers are few and are difficult to identify. Moreover, the corporation may need clearance from the Department of Justice before it can set a price or accept a definitive offer.

Another inhibiting factor may be management's concern about how the stock market will interpret the action. If the senior executives reach the conclusion that the interpretation is likely to be unfavorable, they will be encouraged to delay until they prepare the financial community to interpret their prospective move in a more favorable light.

This chapter has identified the linkages between structure and decision making in a large corporation and the decision-making behavior of the key executives and middle managers who provide the intelligence, knowledge, and direction that enable the corporation to function and prosper. Our focus has been on how the established mechanisms of organizational response must constantly be modified as markets shift, niches weaken, and profits decline. We noted that all decisions and actions in a large corporation occur through the mediation of top and middle managers, each of whom must balance two roles: his corporate responsibilities and his career objectives. Often they coincide; on many occasions, however, they are in conflict. The chapters that follow shift the center of attention directly to managerial behavior and in the process elucidate how changes in its human resources policy can help the corporation cope more effectively with problems of scale.

7

Scale and
Managerial Behavior

We are now face to face with our central concern—how does corporate scale affect the behavior of managerial personnel? While we can talk, as economists are wont to do, about such abstractions as the large corporation, the market, revenues, and profits, these abstractions assume a reality only as individuals on the corporate hierarchy, from the chief executive to the most recently hired executive trainee, act and react concretely and specifically to internal and external stimuli.

The *Fortune* 500 companies differ among themselves in their human resources policies and procedures. But their similarities are substantial enough to enable us to treat the large corporation as a prototype. Thus these companies' practices with respect to the recruitment, training, assignment, promotion, and retirement of their personnel have a great deal in common. The same is true of functions of the chief executives, the process of corporate succession, and the relationship of the chief executive officer to his board of directors.

We note in passing that the use of the pronoun "he" in

discussing chief executives is more than a matter of style and tradition. As a recent lead article in *Fortune* (April 16, 1984) made clear, with the exception of Katherine Graham of the Washington Post Company, there is no female CEO among the *Fortune* 500 companies or in the line of succession. Although the article explored a range of alternative explanations, none carried more conviction than the reminder that women had entered the executive suite only a decade or so ago and the succession process requires more time. Just as the substantial similarities among large corporations enable us to deal with them as prototypical procedures, so they will enable us, in chapter 9, to develop an agenda for reducing the adverse impact of scale on managerial behavior.

In the first two decades following the war—decades we earlier designated as the Golden Age—most large U.S. corporations were able to accomplish very successfully three interrelated goals. They grew and diversified, in order to take advantage of the rapidly expanding markets at home and abroad. They modified their organizational structures and decision-making processes, to cope effectively with the additional complexities introduced by scale and diversity. And, perhaps most important of all, they provided opportunities for large numbers of able and energetic young executives to pursue corporate careers.

As we have seen, the period since the late 1960s brought increasing volatility and recession. Corporations that had reorganized to cope more effectively with growth experienced strain and tension in confronting the external environment. This structure-market misalignment was paralleled by even greater conflicts that had begun to emerge between the human resources policies of the corporations and the attitudes and behavior of their managerial personnel.

Ultimately, the sustained prosperity of both the United States and its leading corporations was spearheaded by the remarkable changes, both quantitative and qualitative, in the nation's human resources in the years since 1930. An important question that has surfaced recently is whether organizational responses to scale are resulting in the increasing dysfunction of corporate managers. We have seen how organizational structures and employment practices evolved in response to efforts to manage and control enterprises of increasing size. Human resources policies enable corporate leadership to organize, motivate, and manage the work force. They are designed to achieve purposeful, collective effort in the face of the division of labor and specialization that are the foundations for organizing and accomplishing corporate tasks. In the large corporation of today, employees function under conditions of narrow task assignments, tight supervision, and rewards that are only loosely linked to individual or group performance. Clearly, to create a corporate environment that facilitates a high level of individual and collective performance is a major challenge. The challenge is that much greater if new entrants into the corporate environment have grown up with values that lead them to distrust authority, pursue individual life-styles, and search for continuing self-development. The evidence suggests that in most large enterprises, current human resources policies are producing suboptimal results.

The climate for work is determined by the organizational structure within which employees function and by the personnel policies and practices that govern the administration of the work force. Let us therefore look more closely at the nature and implications of changing organizational structures.

The Structural Evolution of the Large Corporation

Up to the 1920s, large business enterprises in the United States were dominated by a senior management group supported by a second level of managers with responsibility for important business functions. Typically these functional responsibilities extended to production, marketing and sales, finance, and engineering. As the size of American enterprises increased, in response primarily to the growth of the national market, the weaknesses of a "centralized, functional, departmentalized operating company structure" became increasingly evident. The burden of coordinating proliferating functional activities made it impossible for senior managers to both control operations and deal effectively with critical issues of strategy, resource allocation, and control.

As Alfred Chandler and others have shown, the answer to this problem of structural dysfunction—pioneered by DuPont, Sears, and General Motors, among others—was to adopt a multidivisional form of organization. Senior management was supported by a small, analytic staff, and business activities were organized around several relatively freestanding operating divisions. These divisions, structured along product, geographic, or customer lines, were organized to be as independent as possible—controlling their own manufacturing, distribution, and personnel. This new organizational form became more widely diffused after World War II and emerged as the predominant organizational model by the 1960s.

These changing organizational concepts served American enterprise well, making it easier for firms to exploit market opportunities during the economic expansion from the end of World War II to the early 1970s. The new structure facilitated the establishment of a workable system of checks and balances among senior management, the corporate staff, and the divisional line managers. Senior management, supported by the corporate staff, focused on strategy and policy, resource allocation, and controls. With the aid of financial accounting and internal MIS systems, senior management could monitor divisional profit performance and could pursue aggressively decisions to invest, acquire, or divest. The corporate leadership was able to function along the lines of an internal capital market, supporting businesses with superior performance and disinvesting or liquidating substandard divisions.

At the operating level, line managers assumed most of the

Scale and Managerial Behavior

direct responsibilities for day-to-day activities. They had authority for most of the functions that produced the business results in their divisions. Sustained by the buoyant business conditions of the time, overall performance by American corporations was generally good, and managers and employees were rewarded generously.

In this period of sustained growth top management resorted to a variety of rewards. First and most important perhaps was rapid promotions. Able young executives were often advanced one or more rungs every two years, and each time made significant gains in terms of income, benefits, and perks.

As a recent article in *Fortune* (March 19, 1984) emphasized, "in cash compensation, American executives up and down the corporate ladder generally make more than their foreign counterparts." Only the West Germans and the Swiss pay upper-middle managers as well as U.S. corporations.

The article goes on to point out that American managers have also had more opportunity to get rich: their compensation plans have long included stock options, which were particularly valuable in the rising stock market of the postwar decades.

Despite its success, the multidivisional organization structure had certain weaknesses, which slowly became manifest. As large corporations grew ever larger, more diversified, and more global, the relatively simple organizations of the 1950s and 1960s evolved into increasingly complex organizations. There were now multiple levels of middle management seeking to forge and strengthen their roles in the decision-making processes. The adverse implications were particularly evident in the increased amount of time required to reach a decision.

Some corporations therefore began to experiment with a matrix type of structure. This approach was tried particularly by large corporations that recognized the need to economize on certain scarce human resources, such as research and development personnel, whose innovative and support contributions were required by several divisions.

145

As the term suggests, matrix management is predicated on managers' having multiple lines of responsibility and reporting. In addition to his line superior, a middle manager might look to a senior engineer for technical supervision and to the head of the R&D department for guidance with respect to new product development. The matrix system also encourages heavy reliance on ad hoc groups, which bring together managers from many different divisions to work on a specific urgent problem; as soon as the solution is developed, or it becomes clear that no solution will be forthcoming, the group dissolves and the members return to their home bases. The president of Intel, Andrew S. Grove, is a strong proponent of the matrix approach (see his recent book, *High Output Management,* [New York, 1983]).

However, the matrix approach also ran into problems. *Business Week* (March 19, 1984) has the following to say in an article on "How Xerox Speeds Up the Birth of New Products": "One key change involves decision-making. Xerox executives now freely admit that the company had strangled itself with a matrix organization. The heads of groups such as product planning, design, service and manufacturing were based in Rochester, N.Y., but reported to separate executives at corporate headquarters in Stamford, Connecticut. . . . The groups had endless debates . . . and no one had priority for getting the products out."

The challenge of an optimal organizational structure for a rapid growth economy had not been satisfactorily resolved when the postwar bull market came to an end in the early 1970s. The world economy went into a period of slow growth, increasing rates of inflation, and intensified competition—conditions that in varying degrees have continued to the present. The experience of the "down market" created the need of top management for more formal, comprehensive controls.

Significant organizational changes occurred during the post–World War II period of rapid expansion in response to shifts in the external and internal environments. One of the most important was the explosive growth of the initially small corporate

Scale and Managerial Behavior

staff positioned between top management and the operating divisions. This development in turn encouraged the divisions to expand their staffs as a buffer from constant inquiries from those at the top.

Paralleling the expansion of these corporate staffs was the breakdown in the operating autonomy of the line divisions. Many relatively freestanding divisions found that much of their earlier authority and responsibility had been fragmented and diffused to new coordinating units at regional or central head-quarters. The leaders of American corporations have never been clear about the right way to organize a divisional business. As noted, divisions may be set up according to geographic regions, product concepts, or customer markets. Many corporations have used all three principles in varying degrees.

Anticipated economies of scale and the need for tightened control in a down market environment encouraged many large corporations to establish centralized functional responsibility in production, marketing, and finance. Usually, these companies vested an increasing degree of authority in the senior managers responsible for these functions. There is always a ready rationale for further centralized functions based on the perceived need to improve cost-effectiveness and/or to achieve better control of operations.

The advances in computer-communications technology un-questionably contributed to this "recentralization." It became relatively easy, reliable, and inexpensive to put in place new computer systems that enabled top management to stay informed on a daily, hourly, often instantaneous basis of important developments in the field.

Corporate leaders perceived effective management of a large, large, diversified enterprise to require more formal controls, more uniformly documented policies, and rigorously defined operating procedures to assure that all business units stay within appropriate limits of risk. Quantifiable economies of scale also sanctioned progressive centralization of important functions; serving the same customer with a number of product lines in different geographic markets often necessitated structural adaptations that cut across the responsibilities of operating business units. The need to orchestrate and coordinate the activities of several businesses within geographic markets, particularly abroad, required management and control structures organized around the territorial markets in which the firm competed. The desiderata of product integrity and product competitiveness necessitated strong central oversight governing R&D, product development, and management of the firm's principal product lines. In varying degrees, all large corporations reflected these pressures in their organizational realignments.

These developments all tend to reduce business autonomy at the operating level, complicate decision making, add to the complexity of corporate procedures, and reinforce bureaucratic trends. Most important, they have the paradoxical effect of diffusing power while aiming at tighter controls at the top. Very few decisions of consequence are left to the sole discretion of the managers of operating departments or divisions. By the end of the 1970s, most large corporations were confronted by serious problems of top-heavy bureaucracy, inefficiency, and loss of managerial accountability and motivation.

The following analysis aims to explore the human resources implications of the structural developments we have just summarized. While there is a superficial rationality to the organizational structure of most large corporations, a closer inspection reveals that there are many negative aspects that have detrimental consequences for the human beings who are employed and, by extension, threaten the long-term profitability and viability of the corporation. If the collective skills and intelligence of the work force are not utilized productively or enhanced, the corporation, as a competitive economic enterprise, will in time be at risk. When we consider the interaction between structure and people in a large organization, human resources issues are important because they are decisive for the firm's capacity to achieve its basic purpose—to earn a profit and to create value for its owners.

Human Resources Implications

There is considerable literature on the issue of the basic purpose of a large corporation. Some, like Milton Friedman, believe that this is a false issue since the beginning and end of a business is to earn profits for the stockholders. But the validity of this approach is questionable once one lengthens the horizon during which profits can be realized and pays attention to the complex of actors who can affect the outcome. Thus, the alternative view, which commands wider allegiance, recognizes as "stakeholders" not only stockholders, but also managers, other employees, trade unions if the work force is organized, suppliers, dealers, customers, and the people living in communities in which the corporation has a major presence. The profits that a corporation is able to earn over the longer term depend in large measure on its ability to establish and maintain effective relations with all of the stakeholders. No large corporation can afford to ignore the interests of the stakeholders even if it must, from time to time, act against one or more of them in order to protect and advance its own objectives.

We recognize and acknowledge the importance of the concept of the stakeholder. However, to simplify our analytic schema, we will focus on the central purpose of a business enterprise, which is a business purpose—value creation, as validated in the marketplace. Thus policies and practices relating to organization and employee performance are good if they enhance the value-creating results and value-creating potential of the enterprise; they are bad policies and practices if they do not.

As discussed, present policies and practices essentially combine tight controls at the top, splintering of power among different staff divisions, and only limited autonomy for operating divisions. This combination creates an environment in which managers at all levels of the hierarchy become increasingly preoccupied with concerns other than resource utilization and the enhancement of revenues. They have no option but to direct a large amount of energy and effort to playing the game as it is played in most large corporations. And play the game they do. Junior managers modify their work habits and behavior to bring them into line with the expressed and implied preferences of immediate supervisors, whose appraisals will affect their future progress in the company. At all levels—junior, middle, as well as senior— managers adopt a style of work that contributes to smooth relations with their peers on whose cooperation they must depend. And at all levels, managers spend considerable time seeking out and exchanging information about the changing positions of key individuals and groups. Such efforts go beyond simple curiosity. Up-to-date information can protect a manager from ending up on the wrong side, backing a loser. For example, in a conservative organization such as DuPont one could observe that in a three-hour meeting no one spoke out of turn; the senior person always spoke first, the most junior last.

These behavior patterns are all at variance with the central purpose of the corporation—to earn a profit. A bureaucratized enterprise comes to behave more like a political organization, dealing in power, than a business organization, dealing in economic value.

We need to look once again at "the cushion," which does so much to create and maintain a sense of security among all members of the managerial hierarchy. The cushion testifies to the long-term successful performance of the corporation, demonstrating that it has learned to navigate successfully in a dynamic economy. Further, it is a source of comfort to top managers, who need not respond to each shift in the market;

Scale and Managerial Behavior

one of the advantages of a large cushion is the protection it affords the corporation and its top management against short-term adversity.

The cushion also affects the behavior of middle management. The fact that they spend so much time and effort seeking to improve their internal relations, rather than fighting for more business and higher profits, reflects their perception that the corporation's strong market position will help insure that they and their division will meet their business goals. As these attitudes and behavior patterns solidify, they come to affect every important activity and slowly drain the economic vitality of the corporation. We can illustrate this by analyzing the negative consequences of the corporate climate on the work and goals of the individual manager.

Most large corporations follow a basically similar approach to organizing their portfolio of operating businesses. Typically these operating business units are led by professional middle managers, who are seeking advancement up the corporate hierarchy. The capital required to support these businesses is "allocated" from the central corporate capital pool, and the expected return on that capital is measured by the corporate MIS. The cost of such capital is defined by internally established rates, which reflect the corporate leadership's judgment of a desired rate of return, or by some cost factor reflecting corporate experience in raising long-term funds in the capital markets. Sometimes capital costs are not assigned or not fully assigned to profit centers since they are considered a "noncontrollable" variable. Capital charges may be relatively stable or frequently altered, depending, for example, on whether top management wants to reflect changes in the external costs of capital, increase or decrease the reported profitability of particular divisions, or elicit a desired behavior on the part of a division.

In the individual business unit, the existing product lines are not readily changed. The opportunity to alter product offerings is limited, in many cases severely, by views and opinions of other management units. Critical resources—production facilities, additional financial resources, access to the corporate sales force—are frequently under the control of other management units. The same problem faces an operating division that seeks to gain broader access to such resources as premises, computers, and advertising. In the representative large corporation, the cost of these noncontrolled resources are allocated to the operating units through decisions at the top that are entered into the corporate MIS. In most cases, such cost allocation determinations are subjective to some, often to a considerable degree, since it is not possible to measure in an objective manner the appropriate costs to be assigned to each of the operating units. These noncontrolled costs, usually including a measure of corporate overhead, are in effect often only loosely related to real values determined in the marketplace. In the corporate environment, the operating managers occupy the role of an "internal user" or "customer" of the centralized resource base. The operating manager is constrained to negotiate internally over availability and quality of noncontrolled resources but with little and sometimes no leverage as to price, quality, or timeliness.

To a lesser but still notable degree, the shadow pricing that is used to determine the costs of goods as they move from one to another stage in the procurement-production-distribution cycle also is characterized by more or less arbitrary determinations made by people at the top. In many large corporations the difficulty of establishing reasonable shadow prices has been recognized. Thus subsidiary managers have been permitted to buy part of what they need in the market or else given a prominent voice on the committee that establishes the shadow prices.

Ken Auletta in *The Art of Corporate Success* (1984) reports that after listening to a detailed presentation by the staff on gains in productivity achieved through improved materials, management, and purchasing, the CEO of Schlumberger remarked: "Since we are selling equipment to ourselves, it is hard

Scale and Managerial Behavior

to measure" (p. 75). There was no competition over price or product or rate of production, he said, and their charts were therefore relatively worthless.

In the large corporation, the operating business is measured by comparing profit/loss results with budgeted goals as defined by the conventions of the management information system. The MIS figures are different from the financial accounting figures that provide the stockholders and financial markets with a picture of the corporation's earnings and assets. For reasons already noted, the MIS contains a much larger number of arbitrary allocations by top management of both costs and revenues to differing profit centers to help control and assess the behavior of operating managers. These MIS numbers and the judgments based on them frequently differ, and often substantially, from the judgments of the marketplace as revealed in the financial accounts about the overall profitability of the firm.

An operating manager's reviews and rewards are based largely on the information developed by the corporate MIS. As a consequence, the fundamental "accountability" of the manager is to higher management whose judgments are not based nor can they be based exclusively on the verdict of the marketplace about the corporation as a whole. Rewards are further determined by corporate policies that set salary levels, bonuses, and other forms of incentive compensation in response to overall corporate earnings. The consequence of this assessment and reward system is that most managers in operating units of the corporation are rewarded on the basis of results that deviate, often considerably, from those that reflect how well their unit is performing if judged by the marketplace.

A well-publicized instance of a problematic decision to distribute bonuses involved General Motors. In 1982, shortly after Roger B. Smith became chairman, 6,000 upper-level managers were given substantial bonuses based on much improved corporate earnings. The timing was poor since GM had just signed a contract with the UAW in which its workers gave back $2.5

billion in wages and benefits. The bonus proposal was quickly withdrawn because of strong trade union and public disapproval.

In the large, bureaucratized corporation, arbitrary allocation policies, highly developed internal controls, and formal procedures for obtaining essential resources through the corporate hierarchy are the prevailing facts of life. The distribution of power and authority makes it necessary for managers of operating units to negotiate with superiors, peers, and subordinates to obtain support on a wide range of decisions and actions. This is a complex process, which consumes a large part of the time and energy of all line managers. These established corporate practices and procedures have the effect of limiting the autonomy and reducing the initiative of line managers, thereby impairing their ability to act quickly and responsively to changes in market conditions. Moreover, this diffusion of authority, which forces all of the operating units into dependent relationships with other line and staff units that control essential resources and sign-off authority, is critical to the operating divisions' performance and well-being.

This organizational environment, with its blurring of responsibility, authority, and accountability, has major implications for the type of leadership that emerges. Necessarily, much of the task of top management in the large corporation involves coordinating, balancing, and arbitrating among various in-house groups. Each of the competing groups controls some scarce resources that others require in order to accomplish their objectives. And in many instances a group holds out, seeing a greater advantage in noncooperation than in assisting the operating division that is seeking its help.

A recent article in the *Wall Street Journal* (February 13, 1984) speaks to the issue; it carried the following lead: "Bell Battles: AT&T Marketing Men Find Their Star Fails to Ascend as Expected—Manufacturing Experts Win Early Rounds in the Clash of Corporate Cultures." The long article explains that "marketing executives and manufacturing veterans are locked

Scale and Managerial Behavior

in a power struggle for control of the company" and that "manufacturers have gained the upper hand." A recently resigned marketing executive is quoted as saying, "It's a clash in corporate cultures that produces battle after battle between these two segments—I'm relieved to be out of all the political turmoil going on at AT&T."

The structural context in which operating units function in the large corporation creates a range of problems that make it difficult for managers (and workers as well) to focus their energies on the primary corporate objective—to create value. Moreover, the distortions are subtle. The many internally created "buffers" to economic reality and the network of dependent power relationships channel a great amount of employee energy into nonproductive activity, which can and often does compromise the wealth-creating capacity of the firm as a whole. These dysfunctional organizational phenomena are aggravated by the human resources policies and practices characteristic of most large corporations; and their combined effects indicate how unsupportive the work environment has become for effectively eliciting the skills and motivation of the large corporation's work force, particularly its managers.

In the representative large corporation, philosophies and policies relating to the management of human resources that have the imprimatur of senior management are readily identifiable. Typically, they affirm the central importance of people to the economic success of the enterprise and embrace the principle of promotion through merit, thus linking career progression and rewards to successful performance on the job. Basic to this "credo" is the concept that employee merit and successful performance relate to the central mission of the enterprise—the economic mission of the creation of value for the stockholder-owners. Employees are explicitly encouraged to identify their jobs and the performance of their duties with this corporate mission. Rewards, promotions, and personal progress are said to flow directly from success—in performance quantitatively measured against economic and other goals and objectives established for the specific jobs.

While a great many large firms proclaim their adherence to a performance-based approach, the evidence suggests otherwise. What actually happens to people in large corporations, in terms of career progression and personal rewards, bears little resemblance to these corporate ideals. We can identify the gaps among intentions, actions, and results by describing the various stages of a prototypical manager's career and identifying where and how slippage occurs.

The Upwardly Mobile Manager

Major corporations approach the recruitment and assimilation of new employees in a more or less similar manner. The recruiting approaches to blue-collar, clerical, and other salaried workers, including management trainees, have a great deal in common however much they may differ in detail. Job applicants in American society seek employment primarily to secure an income, but they also expect opportunities for personal and career development as well as for economic security in retirement. In return, they are prepared to commit time and talent to the performance of their assigned duties, subject to fairly applied disciplines and sanctions on their behavior, and they accept their employer's judgments regarding their continuing suitability for employment and advancement in the organization.

The recruiting process involves preliminary screening of prospective employees by the firm's personnel staff. The interviewer not only evaluates the applicant's competences and potential but also utilizes the recruiting process as a critical opportunity to communicate the corporation's business values and general culture. Applicants are evaluated against a perceived ideal recruit. A person who is viewed as someone who will "fit in" and "get on well" in the corporation, who will be comfortable with "the way we do things," gets the nod. As these selection criteria gain credence and appear to be validated by experience, the large corporation tends to narrow the sources from which prospective employees are sought.

It was conventional wisdom some years past that U.S. Steel preferred to recruit its young engineers from state universities in the Midwest on the theory that many of the students had grown up on the farm and were used to putting in a full day's work starting at 5 A.M.

In the affluent sixties, Procter & Gamble was surprised to find that many of its young salesmen balked when asked to work on Saturdays. The explanation lay in its particular narrow recruitment pattern. Inquiry disclosed that Procter & Gamble was recruiting heavily on the campuses of the Ivy League schools. Many of its recruits—as well as the young women to whom these young managers were married—were used to spending weekends at their parents' country clubs.

It is difficult to know exactly how much weight and responsibility to assign to the "professionalization" of the personnel function in establishing many of the norms, policies, and procedures that currently dominate the human resources environment in large corporations. But we must not minimize the leverage that the personnel people have come to exert as a result of their success in institutionalizing their function and in developing the hallmark, even the essence, of a distinctive discipline. The influence of the corporate human resources specialists, as they prefer to be known, is pervasive and impacts on all facets of managerial behavior.

The corporate value system first articulated during the recruitment process is solidified during the new employee's orientation and initial training. During this period, essential job skills are taught; more important, great care is taken to emphasize how things are done and how things are not done in the corporation. However, despite often elaborate screening procedures that include repeated interviews, tests, and group appraisal sessions, a high proportion of new personnel, particularly of college graduates, leave the corporation within the first three to five years. If half of all recently hired management trainees are still on the payroll after five years, the recruiters and higher management seem to be satisfied.

Employees hired by operating divisions are usually placed in jobs immediately, and orientation and training occurs subsequently. Other hires go through a period of indoctrination and training, varying from a few days to up to a year, before being assigned. But at some time, the new employee is judged ready to perform useful work and on the basis of an up-to-date appraisal receives his initial assignment.

The next stage of the employee's career is aptly labeled apprenticeship. The first assignment begins the process of the ongoing, on-the-job training that is part of the experience of every employee within one of the operating divisions or within a staff unit. During this period, important peer and mentor relationships develop. The new employee begins to realize that his advancement in the firm will depend not only on his technical performance on the job but also on the quality of his relations with other members of the work group and with those in supervisory roles. He also comes to understand that his future in the firm is directly linked to the future of his work group and division within the corporate hierarchy.

During apprenticeship, the employee has his first real contact with the performance appraisal process. He is judged not only against his specific work goals but also according to such factors as how well he gets along with others, his initiative and intelligence, and his ability as a team player. Rewards and punishments are meted out in accordance with these appraisals. During the apprenticeship period, a considerable winnowing of the new employee population occurs. Many new employees, assessing their experiences and reactions to date, decide to leave. And many more are encouraged by peers and superiors to seek

Scale and Managerial Behavior

another position since they are perceived not "to fit in."

The basic contract between the large corporation and the employee is established during this early period. The employee realizes that he will have the opportunity to learn the skills necessary to perform his expanding duties, and he also learns what is required of him in terms of personal behavior and group loyalty if he is to advance into middle and senior management.

As his years of service increase, the key factor in his mobility is the growth and profitability of the business unit with which he is associated and, particularly, the progress of its leaders within the corporate hierarchy. The ability of his group to position itself competitively over other groups is a key factor in determining whether it will be able to gather intelligence, stake out claims, and command necessary resources to carry out its assignments successfully and on time. As we have seen, power and authority in the large corporation are widely diffused, and consequently, there is constant intracorporate competition, confrontation, and negotiation among the various units that are jockeying for position. Small resource-poor groups constantly face the risk that they will lose out—that power will be taken away from them, that they will be absorbed by larger groups, or even that they will be liquidated.

In this intracorporate competitive game, assignments of responsibility, control over resources, and credit for revenues depend on the bargaining power of the groups within the corporate hierarchy. The performance record of each group at the end of each year will reflect not only how well it used its resources and performed in the marketplace but also how successful it was in holding onto its key people, how well it negotiated with the controllers of the MIS, and how effectively its leadership communicated its successes to top management. In some instances, what is "said" and "heard" has greater weight in the corporate evaluation process than what was actually accomplished in terms of bottom line figures. The more intense and pervasive competition becomes, the greater the likelihood that in high corporate councils, impressions of accomplishment will crowd out, at least for a time, the underlying realities. The ease with which appearance and reality can be confused requires a smart group leadership to spend much of its time and energy with senior management, "presenting" the group's interests and calling attention to its successes. As with other political activities in the corporation, this often occurs at the expense of concrete business tasks that could result in higher profits.

As the employee attains a more responsible position as a member of a larger and more consequential group, the risk of intergroup competition increases for both his group and himself. The stakes are raised. From time to time, the group leaders will perceive that a major initiative might result in a significant enhancement of the group's position but at the expense of other groups. Experienced group leaders understand that a major conflict may be precipitated if they push ahead. And if they make their move and lose, the penalties can be severe. Accordingly, they often choose to play it safe. But even a decision in favor of the status quo is not without risk. Action might have resulted in a significant business gain that would have strengthened the group's long-term market position and enhanced the corporation's profits. For this reason, playing it safe is often no more than trading a short-term risk for long-term vulnerability.

In corporations in which power-related behavior patterns are well established, which means in almost all large corporations, managers spend a great deal of their time and energy trying to keep informed of developments that can affect the future of their groups. They attend many meetings for the sole purpose of insuring that the group's franchise or turf is not reduced. The extent to which they find it necessary to expend energy in such defensive tactics means that they can direct less effort to improving the group's business performance and, ultimately, the profitability of the corporation as a whole.

The moral of such behavior is not lost on junior and middle managers. They soon realize that the evaluation of their work

Scale and Managerial Behavior

by supervisors, peers, and subordinates depends as much upon how they are perceived as on how competently they perform, on politics rather than performance. Such a climate favors cautious organizational maneuvering rather than business risk taking. A business initiative may, if successful, yield significant profits, but if it fails it can lead to sizable losses. Since corporate evaluations often do not distinguish between appearance and reality, the typical manager will often decide that he has less to lose if he plays it safe and does not get tagged as a loser. Moreover, if he were to take the risk and succeed, he would have to deal with the discomfort and often the jealousy of his peers and even his superiors.

The long-range impact of such risk-avoiding behavior can have devastating effects. If young managers are shielded from having to operate in an entrepreneurial environment in which they are held accountable for the resources under their command as well as for the consequences of their decisions, they will move up the hierarchy without ever having been forced to operate in an exposed business setting, in which the market calls the shots.

This same highly charged political climate also defines the way in which senior managers are forced to spend much of their time. Rather than focusing on developing new approaches to strengthening the corporation's position in the marketplace, they are busy adjudicating conflicts among the principal groups, divisions, and staff units, each with its claims for increased responsibilities, resources, and personnel. Since no corporation can function without continuing cooperation among its units, intergroup conflicts must be mitigated and preferably resolved. But inevitably new conflicts arise—and corporate "maintenance" comes to preempt much of the time of senior management.

The ultimate irony is that, despite organizational structures based on decentralization, many important decisions must be made at the top, since only those at the top are in a position to balance the necessary tradeoffs required for a "corporate decision." The diffusion of power among many subsidiary units forces those at the top to make the major decisions. Middle managers who learn that this is the way of corporate life see little point in getting caught up in the process. They realize that they cannot significantly affect the outcome. Accordingly, many seek to avoid the inevitable conflicts and decide instead to concentrate on the routine tasks at hand. De facto centralization of critical decision making is the root cause of the large corporation's difficulty in reacting flexibly and responsively to changes in the marketplace.

Upward mobility in the large corporation becomes more a political process than a reward for superior business performance. Employees seek to hitch their wagon to a star. They search for peer and mentor relationships and other alliances through which they can associate themselves with a "winner" or potential winner. In the ultimate mobility game, the leadership succession, the new CEO is often the winner of the political power game, not necessarily the winner of the business game. In extreme instances, the new CEO may have insufficient business acumen to lead the corporation successfully. If his skills have been honed by years of career progression through a series of assignments in which business skills were subordinated to power skills, he may be inadequately prepared to provide business leadership, particularly in a volatile period.

The ultimate loss brought about by the continuing importance of corporate politics is the degradation of the corporate credo in the eyes of employees. The gap between the promises of a corporation's human resources philosophy and the concrete realities of its managers' career experiences is there for all to see and to endure. Employee motivation to pursue profit-making opportunities as effectively as possible and in the process assume the necessary risks is eviscerated, often destroyed, because all who have eyes and ears perceive that rewards and promotions often follow a different rationale.

Scale and Managerial Behavior

Conclusions

We can now assess the impact of corporate size and scale on the effectiveness with which the large corporation makes use of its human resources. Earlier we noted that as the small and medium-sized corporation expands, it can enjoy significant gains in productivity based on economies of scale that are reflected in substantial and continuing profits. We have demonstrated that, beyond a certain point, size becomes a dysfunctional force by creating an unduly complex structure and flawed decision-making mechanisms. In the present chapter we focused on the ways in which this much more complex structure, with its diffusion of power, distorts the behavior of successive levels of management, from the executive trainee to the CEO.

The diffusion of responsibility and the fragmentation of authority create the preconditions for power-determined behavior among the major business/staff units in the corporation. As this behavior pattern becomes more firmly established, the major groups act increasingly in their own interest to preserve and enhance their position, pursuing goals that often contribute little if anything to improving the present or prospective profits of the corporation.

This behavior pattern increasingly deflects the energies of all levels of management away from business objectives in the marketplace to the pursuit of internal political goals. Senior management, dependent on staff support and confronted with skillful negotiators, is forced to spend more and more of its time arbitrating and adjudicating among intrafirm competitors. Managers learn how to survive in the power game and most of them decide that their best prospect of advancement is to accommodate to the shifting realities within the organization.

When such behavior becomes pervasive, the corporation is genuinely at risk because it can no longer focus its energies on the marketplace, the final source of profits and growth. The question that remains for us to address is whether the large corporation can reduce—even if it cannot totally eliminate—the dysfunctional effects of scale on the utilization of its human resources. Before we address the question of potential remedies, we must look more closely at the role of the chief executive officer, who by action or inaction exercises major influence on all aspects of corporate performance, including the use of human resources.

8

The Chief
Executive Officer

By law, tradition, and fact, the chief executive officer of a large corporation has primary responsibility for insuring the corporation's short- and long-term profitability and growth. He has responsibility for final decision making, internal coordination, and crisis management, as well as for strategic diagnosis and direction setting, succession planning, board relations, and public representation. The enumeration of these responsibilities immediately suggests a potential problem. We cannot expect any individual, no matter how talented, to discharge effectively such a broad range of responsibilities. But this problem comes as no surprise. Most people in major positions of authority and responsibility are overextended; few can give adequate attention to all the issues that reach their desks and identify others before they make their way there.

In light of these realities, true leadership is revealed, first, by the issues to which the executive directs his personal attention and, second, by the quality of his decisions. Both of these criteria dictate how well the organization performs. If the organization meets its goals, the executive will be judged a success; it is a matter of little or no moment whether he was able to attend to and resolve a host of secondary issues.

In fact, however, the CEO's success or failure cannot be assessed by any simple measures of corporate performance. Even a long run of good profits and growing revenues provides no certainty that the chief executive is supplying superior leadership. In retrospect, it is clear that the CEOs of both GM and Ford in the mid and late 1970s failed to appraise correctly many of the changes in the international markets that would place their corporations under pressure in the 1980s by replacing profits with losses.

Although the conventional measures—corporate profits and revenue growth—provide a basis for judging the effectiveness of the chief executive's performance, they have a number of serious limitations. Among these we will single out three.

First, they do not take account of the condition of the corporation at the time of the CEO's appointment. If the firm were making little or no profits, it would be unreasonable to expect a new chief executive to reach the average for his industry after a year or two in office.

Second, since macro conditions have a major influence on both corporate profits and growth, a radical change in the economic environment must be factored into any performance test. In good times most CEOs look good because most companies are making profits and enjoying substantial rates of growth. In bad times it is difficult even for a talented CEO to do much better than break even, particularly if his is a cycle-sensitive business.

The third limitation is both more complex and more important. These conventional measures do not assess how well the CEO is positioning the corporation for future growth and long-term profitability. This is at once the most crucial and, as we shall see, the most demanding of the CEO's responsibilities, although

The Chief Executive Officer

it often loses out in the competition with the other functions for his attention.

Typically, the CEO is an individual who has progressed up the organizational hierarchy, usually after years of working in the corporation he has come to head. He expects to lead the corporation for ten to fifteen years until his retirement, when he hopes to pass honorably into the hall of former corporate leaders. The CEO assumes a duty to preserve and increase the corporation's net worth and has at least a partial vision of how to accomplish this objective.

However, the issue of leadership is more complex and extends far beyond the preservation and enhancement of the corporation's assets. A large business enterprise is never static; it is either expanding or declining. And expansion or decline is reflected in the market worth of the company as it changes over time, that is, the earnings of the corporation now and an estimate of its future earnings. The CEO's most important responsibility is to know the market worth of his company and to improve that worth during the tenure of his leadership. Unfortunately, there are real obstacles to his accomplishing what is at one and the same time a simple and a difficult task. Accounting conventions and regulatory specifications do not require businesses to "mark the company to market." Consequently, in most sectors of the economy, there are often buried or unrecognized assets and/or liabilities in the balance sheet.

A recent *Business Week–Harris Executive Poll* (February 20, 1984) asked executives "whether they believed that the stock market accurately reflected the company's real value." Only 32 percent were content with the valuation; 60 percent had "a real sense of grievance." Of the remainder, 6 percent were not sure and only 2 percent believed that their company was overvalued. The poll went on to point out that this pervasive undervaluation by the stock market helped to explain the large number of recent divestitures. The CEOs who were selling off divisions with little or no earnings expected the stock market to take a more optimistic view of their future earnings.

The CEO's Responsibility

The first priority of the CEO, then, is to diagnose his corporation realistically, to ascertain whether it is expanding or contracting, and to understand which units are contributing positively, and which negatively, to its overall economic performance. As we have seen, successful businesses tend to pass through distinct stages: early rapid expansion, mature but slower growth, a plateau, and then decline. At the same time, each business is influenced by the fluctuations in the economy at large: cyclical recovery of the economy usually follows a short or long period of recession.

It is not easy, even for an astute CEO, to distinguish clearly between a condition of reduced profits or even losses brought about by a cyclical downturn and a structural change where the unfavorable developments bespeak a long-term loss of corporate competitiveness. One of the reasons that many CEOs do not slough off a division when it shows signs of slippage is their expectation that the market will shortly right itself and that when it does, the division will again earn profits. Even if a CEO understands the marketplace, he may be unable or unwilling to act. He may still hope that time will eliminate the necessity for radical intervention, whether in the form of large new investments to modernize a faltering division or divestiture. Either form of intervention could have negative overtones. He may have to borrow to make the additional investments; and if he divests he would signal stockholders and the stock market that the corporate asset figure on his balance sheet might have to be reduced.

A business enterprise that has reached significant scale may soon be entering a phase of moderating growth or prospective decline. Thus, it becomes especially important that the CEO correctly diagnose the true state of affairs of the various parts of his corporation. His diagnoses and subsequent actions will help determine the potential of the enterprise as a whole to survive and continue to prosper.

For a variety of reasons—historical, institutional, and environmental—CEOs find it difficult to undertake effectively this diagnostic task. But unless they do, their decisions, whether related to short-term or long-term goals, will almost certainly be flawed. Every CEO is to some degree a captive of his earlier experiences. He sorts out those responses that have served him well in the past and relies on them to guide him in the future. Since most CEOs reach the top only after long service, they tend to place great weight on policies and procedures that they have followed and that have proved themselves.

General Motors and its CEOs in the late 1960s and 1970s (Donner, Gerstenberg, and Murphy), had learned their lessons well. The American public liked big, comfortable cars, and selling such cars was the best way for GM to continue to make large profits. They had noted the steep rise in the price of gasoline after OPEC became operational in the early 1970s, and they were aware of the increased number of imported cars. But they discounted these developments and continued in their accustomed ways, convinced that history was a trustworthy guide. After all, GM had been making profits since the early 1920s. The most reasonable assumption, and the one that senior management favored, was that the American public would continue to devote a large part of its discretionary income to the purchase of large cars.

The influence of past success on present behavior is hard to overestimate even when top management is engaged in planning for the future. In the early 1960s, DuPont undertook an elaborate exercise in which its top management was exposed to a distinguished group of outside experts, including several Nobel Laureates, whose assignment was to sketch the environment that DuPont was likely to confront two decades later. The experts made a number of proposals, in areas including human resources policies. Corporate executives acknowledged that many of these proposals were reasonable and worth implementing but added that the company was unlikely to put any of them into effect. Those at the top gave heavy weight to the fact that their established policies and procedures had been repeatedly tested and had proven themselves. In the face of this experience they were unwilling to experiment with the new and the untried. True, the new might prove superior, but then again it might not. A cautious management saw no point in assuming an unnecessary risk and therefore decided to stay with what it knew.

Since most people, including CEOs, are shaped by their prior experiences, top management typically relies upon the past to project the future. For example, based on strong early postwar expansion, Ralph Cordiner, the CEO of General Electric, in the 1950s expected his company to grow in sales and profits at around 10 percent per annum far into the future. A review of GE's performance between 1965 and 1981 is revealing. After the inflationary factor is taken into account, sales rose by 2.7 percent, net income after taxes by 3.0 percent, and assets by 3.4 percent. While this record may have surprised and disappointed Ralph Cordiner, GE's own economists had long realized that given its size and scope, GE would find it difficult to outpace the growth of the U.S. economy. This consideration probably goes a fair distance to explain why the current CEO of GE has stated that his long-range strategy is to reduce the number of distinct businesses in which the company is involved and to remain only in those where it is number one or two.

To provide themselves with some simplified guides and guidelines, chief executives have long paid close attention to several ratios used by financiers and investors to make preliminary assessments of a corporation's financial health. These include return on assets, profits per share, debt-to-equity ratio, and cash flow, among others. Many believe that following these criteria is sound business practice.

These criteria of sound financial management also provide CEOs with a useful decision-making framework when operating divisions make competing demands for additional capital. But a financial strategy is not the same as a corporate strategy, and many corporations have lost competitive position, profits, and opportunities for accelerated growth as a result of their CEOs' adherence to simplified, conservative financial criteria. The arrival and persistence of high-level inflation further undermined the value of such financial criteria as a guide for corporate strategy. On February 25, 1984, an article in *The Economist* presented four figures for the profits (after tax and net of interest) of Britain's large manufacturing and distributing companies for the year 1976. These figures ranged from a gain of £4.5 billion to a loss of £1.1 billion! The article called attention to the fact that the low figures were a result of executives' concentrating on maintaining the wrong sort of capital. "Companies are not in business to make widgets but to make money. They need not maintain physical capital.... Shareholders entrust companies with cash: the manager's job, says 'the financial capital school,' is to maintain the general purchasing-power of this cash and if possible to enhance it."

The substantially shortened tenure of CEOs in the last twenty years was the subject of a cover story in *Business Week* (December 19, 1983) based on the work of Professor Eugene Jennings of Michigan State University, a longtime student of empirical trends affecting top management. According to the *Business Week* story, there was a threefold increase in the annual turnover rate among CEOs between 1960–1968 and 1980–1983—from slightly over 3 percent to just under 10 percent. The article offers three principal explanations for this sizable increase: the accelerated number of acquisitions, mergers, and takeovers; the diminishing tolerance of boards of directors for poor performance; and the preference of boards, especially in the high-tech sector, for younger CEOs. One conclusion appears unequivocal: as the economy becomes more volatile and more large corporations are at risk, the CEO whose performance begins to slip can no longer expect to remain in office until conventional retirement age.

Untoward trends in the external economic environment—intensified worldwide competition, inflation, slower growth rates, and unprofitable acquisitions—have individually and collectively multiplied the challenges that confront the CEO of a large corporation. Institutional and environmental forces frequently compound his difficulties.

On the institutional side, for example, a new CEO has often had little opportunity to hone his business, as distinct from his organizational, skills or to demonstrate how he will respond to the radical shifts in the marketplace. There is no way for a CEO of a major corporation to avoid making many critical business decisions—when to invest, how much, in what, when to disinvest, whether to buy or develop new technology, which markets to enter and from which to withdraw. These business decisions are the essence of his work and will sooner or later account for his success or failure. Of course, no CEO can make these decisions alone; he must elicit sound advice from his subordinates, and spur them to speedy and successful implementation once decisions have been reached.

A recent survey of the CEOs of *Fortune* 500 companies revealed that many of the incumbents had been advanced into the top position from a previous senior staff role as chief finance or legal officer. This route to the top suggests that many CEOs had not been in a line position where they had to make business decisions every hour of every day. Certainly no CEO has had all the prior experience that he can profitably use. One of the hallmarks of the successful CEO is his ability to fill the important lacunae in his background and his skill by identifying associates who can reinforce and support him.

No chief executive of a large organization today is the master of his own time and energy, able to use them as he sees fit. Moreover, given the way the large corporation is structured, with constant jockeying for power and resources among its operating divisions and vis-à-vis corporate headquarters, the CEO cannot escape from the role of chief arbiter. No one except the man at the top—or occasionally his alter ego, the chief operating officer, who may be able to resolve the less contentious issues—has the authority, respect, and control over rewards and punishments necessary to moderate the internecine fights that erupt and must be solved.

But no sooner has the CEO settled one issue than other issues are making their way to his desk, and again he alone can handle them. Since a large corporation operates in an unstable environment, its divisions are constantly confronting new opportunities and dangers that they cannot resolve on their own. The divisions must therefore turn to corporate headquarters for approval and support. The senior management team, however, finds itself unable to respond affirmatively to all, or even to most, of the proposals that the divisions develop. To complicate matters further, many of the proposals forwarded to the top are to some degree conflicting.

In such an environment, the CEO must devote much time and energy to what we have called "corporate maintenance," keeping the several divisions pointed toward the market to increase their sales and profits and to moderate their infighting with one another and with corporate headquarters. This is a time-consuming, energy-absorbing task that no CEO, even if he wants to, can avoid. The CEO is held responsible for the operating results of the company, and these are significantly affected by the way in which conflicts and confrontations are handled and resolved.

The wear and tear associated with corporate maintenance helps to explain why many CEOs attempt to lower the level of tensions by resorting to delays in many critical decisions in the hope that time will bring a cure or that their successor, rather than they, will have to take decisive action. Since a successful large corporation has a sizable cushion, it can keep a faltering unit alive. Most CEOs are loath to act precipitously to put a large established unit on the block, partly because they are concerned with the potential effects on morale in the rest of the organization when they cut loose a considerable number of middle and higher level managers who have spent years in the service of the corporation that is now cutting them off. A second source of concern is that the liquidation or sale will be seen as their failure even though the basic difficulties may have predated their term in office.

When the external environment is volatile, when the overall economy and the industry in which the corporation is centered are in flux, the CEO is under increasing pressure to find an appropriate balance between continuing with proven approaches and discarding or modifying some of them in favor of new ways of coping more effectively with changing markets and technology.

In periods of increasing turmoil each CEO looks to other leading corporations in the hope that he can profit by adopting some of their responses. In this regard, many CEOs follow the practice of others, such as business analysts and stockbrokers, who are forced to take positions despite an unknown and uncertain future. They try to hedge their bets.

There is ample evidence of this tendency. For example, a random sampling of the annual reports of major U.S. corporations in 1980–1981 reveals that in a striking number of cases top management had decided to protect the corporation against steeply rising energy costs by acquiring energy companies. Many CEOs, especially of companies that were heavy energy users, decided that if so many of their colleagues considered the purchase of an oil company to be a sound investment, they had better follow suit.

One of the stories making the rounds in Wall Street is that the newly appointed head of a major industrial corporation that was locked into an industry whose future looked particularly

The Chief Executive Officer

bleak decided, largely on his own, to go out and purchase an oil company. While his decision on the surface appears questionable, it may have been justified in the light of the following: the CEO was convinced that a significant acquisition in a new industry was mandatory; his financial advisers were able to make a sound evaluation of the company to be acquired; and discussion and delay would probably have pushed up the purchase price and thus endangered the deal.

When a major corporation such as IBM or AT&T gets entangled with the Department of Justice, federal regulatory bodies, or Congress, the outcome can have a truly revolutionary impact on its future. Accordingly, the CEO and frequently other senior executives have no option but to devote a great deal of time and effort to design bargaining strategies to assure the corporation's future even if, as in the case of AT&T, dismemberment could not be avoided. The conventional wisdom is that the more aggressive posture of IBM in 1983–1984 across all markets, including the personal computer, reflects the favorable resolution of its exhausting antitrust case, which had preempted so much of the attention of senior management throughout most of the 1970s.

But there are also other reasons why CEOs of large corporations cannot afford to neglect the Washington scene. The legislators who draft the tax code, the officials in various regulatory agencies and commissions, and the officials in strategic departments like State, Defense, and Treasury, can all have an impact, for better or worse, on the well-being of even the largest of the nation's corporations. Professor Uwe Reinhardt of the Princeton Economics Department gives a lecture early in his course in elementary economics in which he explains that there are three, and only three, sources of profits for the large corporation: to make and sell widgets better than its competitors; to make all business decisions with an eye to the tax code; and to reduce the number of potential competitors by lobbying in Washington. A recent CEO of General Electric remarked that he was spending more time in Washington than in the corporation's headquarters in Fairfield, Connecticut.

As we have seen, another institutional imperative, very much to the fore in recent years, is that the CEO assume the role of "crisis manager." In the face of shrinking market demand, often associated with shrinking market shares, the P&L statement and the balance sheet can very quickly turn from good or satisfactory to poor or bad. If the financial situation is bad, the CEO must step in and concentrate in his own hands much of the authority for day-to-day operations which had been released in more halcyon days to the field and to staff divisions. An alert CEO will move quickly when early signs point to the market's weakening and/or new competitors make their appearance. In the face of an unfavorable trend, when tomorrow is likely to be worse than today, a CEO who delays in taking over the reins may place the corporation in jeopardy. Often a new CEO must be installed before major corporate problems are analyzed and losses confronted, and then a major earnings decline, a bankruptcy filing, or a takeover appears to occur "out of the blue." The institutional context in which CEOs operate, however, foreshadows such periodic traumatic events.

A number of environmental factors that have surfaced in recent years have added further to the complexities of the CEO's responsibilities. The last decade has witnessed the growth of "professional" management critics, who thrive on asking embarrassing questions at the corporation's annual meeting. The questions embrace both internal and external affairs. These critics often complain about excessive compensation arrangements for senior executives, and they second-guess decisions about offers from the outside that were either rejected or accepted. Occasionally, they stumble onto questionable management practices, for which they insist on an explanation. If not satisfied with that explanation, they may start a court action. And they will also ask why the corporation still has investments in South Africa, why women and minorities are not better

The Chief Executive Officer

represented on the board, and other questions bearing on the behavior of the corporation.

For the most part, these increasingly raucous annual meetings add only a modest burden to the harrassed chief executive, in terms of time spent preparing to cope with prospective hecklers. But if the critics succeed in unearthing evidence of faulty decision making, the consequences can be much more time consuming.

Another recent development relates to this country's highly sophisticated financial markets and its large number of entrepreneurs who are continually looking for opportunities to use their brains and money to make a killing. This development, a somewhat paradoxical one, can be stated as follows: Competent or even superior performance by a CEO and his team is no guarantee that their corporation will not be the target of an unfriendly takeover.

The following paragraphs from the Letter to Stockholders from the CEO and the president of Gulf Oil (*Annual Report, 1983*) provide a vivid if abbreviated account of one such unfriendly takeover effort:

> This should have been the most optimistic letter we have written to shareholders in many years. All of the programs which we have undertaken in the past two years to enhance shareholder value came together during 1983 and are working well. Net income rose 17 percent on a per-share basis to $5.83—almost a billion dollars in total earnings—and we increased our dividend payout for the tenth consecutive year. . . .
>
> Yet despite this success, or perhaps ironically because of it, we are faced with the gravest crisis in your Company's 83-year history. For the past six months, we have been engaged in a bitter fight with a group of opportunists, led by T. Boone Pickens of Mesa Petroleum Co., who are bent on seeing the Company bought out at a high price or wresting control of it for themselves in order to break it apart and sell the pieces for a quick gain. . . .
>
> While we, too, would have preferred to remain independent, and find it difficult to accept that the nation's ninth largest industrial

company and fifth largest oil company can be forced into a merger because of the financial speculations of others, we nevertheless welcome an association with Socal.

The complex maneuvers that led William Agee, CEO of Bendix, to attempt to swallow Martin Marietta, and its counter-move to turn the table on Bendix, which was eventually taken over by Allied, set a new high in corporate jousting. Agee was soon forced out of Allied, and Martin Marietta, carrying a much heavier debt burden, was able to retain its independence.

Most observers of these unfriendly takeovers understand the role played by the CEO of the acquiring company in establishing the strategy, from selecting the victim to winning the battle. But the analysts remain divided in their judgment about the distribution of the gains and losses to the different players, particularly the stockholders of the acquiring and acquired companies.

A couple of examples may help clarify the increasingly pressured role of the CEO under today's volatile conditions. The reasons behind the recent moves of U.S. Steel, first, to pay a large premium for Marathon Oil and, more recently, to seek to acquire National Steel are not easy to reconcile. But perhaps these noncongruent approaches are best seen as moves by a determined CEO to move quickly to reposition U.S. Steel so that it would have better prospects of conserving its assets, diminished in recent years by overextended, outmoded, and poorly located plants. The current CEO does not have the luxury that his predecessors believed they had of waiting for the steel market to right itself. The outlook does not favor an early return to an expanding, profitable market. Rather, international competition in steel is likely to intensify.

The decline of International Harvester to a point where it was but a few days away from bankruptcy proceedings had a number of causes. These included a radical downturn in the market, inappropriate product lines, low productivity, intensified competition, and finally, a costly strike, which brought the company to the abyss. It was Archie McCardell's judgment that the company should go to the mat with its powerful union and should not settle until it had won major concessions. This misjudgment—for so it turned out to be in the face of the union's intransigence—cost him his job.

So far we have explored how the changing exigencies of the large corporation have resulted in increasing demands on its chief executive officer. As mentioned in the beginning of this chapter, the CEO's changed role has in turn had some crucial consequences for the corporation's human resources. It is to these consequences that we now turn.

The Pressure of Multiple Demands

Our argument in brief is that because of the inordinate demands that are made on his time and energy, the CEO is hard pressed to devote adequate attention to the corporation's human resources. He can no longer fulfill relevant functions ranging from developing new policies to spotting and helping to develop the firm's managerial talent.

To lighten his own burden and to improve his control over the enterprise, the CEO often establishes new corporate staff functions. These have the effect of enhancing the corporate bureaucracy and proliferating the number of parties at interest in the decision-making process. To ease the burden of conflict resolution, the CEO tends to reward "team players" in the promotion and succession processes. He will often sacrifice the innovative, headstrong, entrepreneurial individuals, who may see more clearly the economic risks and opportunities facing the corporation. To get an "objective" view of the issues causing conflict, the CEO tends to rely on his immediate staff. This tendency reinforces the isolation of his position from the day-to-day realities of the corporation and the reactions of the marketplace to its performance. To get at the "truth" of the business, he permits or sanctions further elaboration of the corporate MIS, which often compounds the difficulties of arriving at a consistent, objective economic view of the business's performance over time. To promote innovation, the CEO often sanctions the creation of new organizational entities, which will share authority with the established units. This adds to organizational complexity and makes the corporation even more difficult to manage.

The rarified atmosphere in which most CEOs operate, the buffers that their staffs erect, and the constraints on their time make it difficult for them to develop an independent basis for judging the capacity and potential of managers two or three rungs down the corporate ladder. Hence in this critical responsibility—the identification and nurturing of managerial talent—the CEO often singles out individuals who have made a good first or second impression on him. Because of time pressure, he is seldom able to accurately judge the manager's potential or to help him develop it. Some years ago top executives of one of the nation's leading chemical companies spent considerable time in visits to their plants, seeking to identify younger and middle managers with potential for superior general or technical performance. Today we seldom hear of such a practice.

We hear even less of a CEO who spends most of his time on corporate human resources. The rarity of the phenomenon is apparent from the following statement by Benno Schmidt, a leading investment banker and a longtime director of Schlumberger, who is appraising Jean Riboud, its CEO: "Riboud spends more time on people and people's problems, in contrast to business and business problems, than any other chief executive I've ever seen. I think the thing he's most concerned with in running this vast business is coming as near as possible to having exactly the right man in the right place all the time. Most people who run a company are much more interested in business, new products, research—all that" (Auletta, *The Art of Corporate Success,* p. 85).

The building up of a personal staff is only one of the ways in which the CEO, in seeking to lighten the burden on himself may, over the long pull, add to his troubles and impede the fuller development of the corporation's human resources. Another difficulty stemming from the top relates to the conflict in goals all CEOs confront—the conflict between optimizing short-term profits and strengthening the corporation's long-term position. An emphasis on short-term profits accounts for the reluctance of division heads to release their most promising people for corporate reassignment, on the ground that the unit's performance will be adversely affected if they do. But without a well-designed corporate management development policy, which necessitates reassignments even at the cost of current profits, there will be an inadequate pool of general managers for senior positions. And this is the pool from which the next CEO is often selected. Unless the CEO recognizes this problem and addresses it, much valuable corporate talent will remain undeveloped. As we have noted, one of the CEO's principal tasks is to keep organizational conflicts, overt or camouflaged, from interfering with collaboration among the several staff and operating divisions. The ubiquity of the conflict mentality, even when it is constrained, helps to explain the preference of the CEO for associates who tend to agree with him, at least most of the time. The man at the top must have some tolerance for dissent, but before he reaches the saturation point he must call a halt. Many CEOs adopt a behavior mode wherein they favor advocates who will handle most of their own problems and, if they seek his opinion, will accept it easily. Relatively few CEOs have the stamina that is required to keep on their team strong persons who will argue for their own views, even if they know that the CEO holds a different opinion.

It is worth digressing for a moment to recognize the conspicuous differences among three of our strongest presidents in recent decades—Roosevelt, Eisenhower, and Johnson—with respect to toleration for dissent among their advisers. Roosevelt enjoyed, encouraged, and presumably profited from disagreements and conflicts among his close advisers. He had the reputation of appearing to agree with each person with whom he talked, but when he made his decision, many advocates who thought they had convinced him found themselves among the losers. In contrast, Eisenhower did not encourage confrontational discussions; this policy applied to all but a select few of his closest advisers. When his successor at Columbia University, on returning from a trip to Southeast Asia, pointed out what he believed to be shortcomings in U.S. policy in the area, Eisenhower responded testily that he should talk with Dulles, who was responsible for foreign policy.

But the most defensive of the presidents was Lyndon Baines Johnson. His lack of tolerance for dissent was especially evident in matters affecting policy in Vietnam following his decision in 1965 to enlarge the U.S. combat role. Until after the Tet offensive, Johnson simply stonewalled all critics. He would not explore any alternative that looked to compromise and withdrawal.

The intellectual and emotional resilience of chief executives to interact on a continuing basis with strong associates who have their own style of acting and reacting to evidence and events may account more than any other factor for the quality of the CEO's performance. This applies not only to the CEO's interaction with staff but also to his relations with the board.

Although the CEO holds his position by virtue of his selection by the board of directors and serves at their pleasure, a chief executive who has had a long and successful period in office often succeeds in dominating his board. In part, this is the result of his influence in selecting new board members, many of whom are either his friends or his subordinates. Most CEOs believe that it is better to keep the board at arm's length. Otherwise, there is a risk that one or more of the board members may raise questions about strategy, operations, and personnel that the CEO would prefer not to discuss, especially not out in the open, with several of his management colleagues present.

The board also finds an arm's-length relationship desirable. Most members are active individuals with heavy demands on their time and energy, and they prefer that their involvement in oversight activities be limited. In normal times, they read summaries of the corporation's current operations and future plans and, when they meet in committee or as a whole, deliberate only selected issues. Unless there is a major warning signal—a precipitous drop-off in earnings, an important lawsuit, or some other untoward development—the directors are likely to follow the CEO's lead and act in a confirmatory and ratifying role. A major insurance company, after several years of lackluster earnings, reported a loss of over $100 million in its property and casualty business. At that point, the board decided to set up a special committee to review monthly the P&L statement.

While there may be a rationale for the CEO's arm's-length relation with his board, it is by no means always a clear-cut gain. In a rapidly changing economic environment, knowledgeable board members can often provide important information, leads, and assessments that can help the CEO chart his long-term strategy. Although it is customary for the CEO to consult with his board, at least with selected members, before deciding to make a bid to acquire a company, in many instances by the time he does so, his planning is already far advanced.

The CEO who consults with his board only on routine matters and spends most meetings informing them of actions taken and prospects for the next quarter may pay a heavy price. If the board includes a number of highly competent persons, the CEO deprives himself and his colleagues of critically important information. A few large R&D corporations have recently resorted to a compromise device. They continue to use a conventional board in a conventional manner. But they also have access to a distinguished group of scientists and technologists, who help them assess their options and formulate responses to the changing technical environment. Many large European companies pay more attention to the quality of their boards of directors and make better use of them. A leading Swedish industrialist recently said, "I have directed particular attention to the board of directors and top management. . . . A key word in this context is 'competence' which is required at all stages and levels because the real world is so many-faceted. The [board] members should, for instance, possess such characteristics as will enable them to have the expertise required to permit efficiency within the company." (*Skandinaviska Enskilda Bank, Quarterly Review,* February 1983).

The former CEO of one of the most successful of U.S. corporations, Dayton Hudson, also has strong views about the importance of the board, its membership, and its responsibilities (*Harvard Business Review,* January/February 1984). "Every time you find a business in trouble, you find a board of directors either unwilling or unable to fulfill its responsibilities. . . . Currently our model calls for a board of 15—with 12 outsiders and 3 members of management. . . . Our executive is made up of all the nonmanagerial members plus the CEO. It is therefore a committee of the whole. . . . The board has the vital role of protecting the corporation's future . . . the board must be independent of management. . . ."

The one unquestioned prerogative of the board is to appoint the CEO. If the corporation is performing satisfactorily, the board is likely to follow the recommendation of the retiring CEO, who usually holds informal conversations with key members to ascertain their views and to discover whether his preferred candidate will be acceptable. The board members assume, understandably, that the current leader is in a better position than they to assess the strengths and weaknesses of those in the running.

However, the fact that so many CEOs do not complete their

terms underscores the fragility of the selection process. We believe this reflects the previously noted preference of many CEOs to choose good team players as senior associates over stronger, more independent managers. When it is time to appoint a new CEO, the small group of eligibles within the company's top cadre may not contain any individual with both broad business experience and leadership potential, especially in light of the "specialist" nature of their earlier assignments. The retiring CEO does not acknowledge this shortcoming and generally would argue that it does not exist. In this way, governance through the board of directors and the process of leadership succession often tend to compound the risk facing the large corporation, until it is too late and sudden, dramatic change becomes inevitable.

One result of the jockeying for position in the period prior to the appointment of a new CEO is that managerial decision making slows down. The key contenders are likely to exercise extreme caution in the year or two preceding the selection. Thus, they do not challenge the incumbent CEO, they do not antagonize any strong operating group, and they do not take unpopular or risky actions. Moreover, after the selection has been made, the unsuccessful candidates are likely to leave, often taking their principal associates with them. The new CEO will usually reward his allies. While these dynamics may be largely inevitable, our point is that they deflect the key players from focusing on the business, on the profit-making activities. Instead, each individual pursues a risk-avoidance posture until the CEO decision has been reached and usually for some time thereafter. In the meantime, long-term strategy, new technology, and emerging competition do not command the attention that they should, to the detriment of the company, its board of directors, and its new CEO.

In cases where the board discovers that its selection was a poor one and asks for the CEO's resignation, a replacement is more likely be sought on the outside. A recent book by Patricia

O'Toole, *Corporate Messiah—The Hiring and Firing of Million Dollar Managers* (1984), recounts a series of cases where boards faced this problem. In most cases, their second choice was no better than their first. The book also discusses a related problem that boards often handle poorly: relieving superannuated chief executives of responsibility. This created difficulties at Polaroid, CBS, ITT, Greyhound, and Occidental.

Conclusions

We can now pull together the several threads of our analysis. Our first finding is that the chief executive's duties have become inordinately complex because of the scale and scope of the large corporation and the fact that by law and practice he is responsible for all aspects of the company's performance, now and in the future.

The second finding is that even as the CEO explores, decides on, and implements actions to strengthen the corporation's position, he must deal with a multiplicity of other demands in order to maintain the corporation as a functioning organization. It devolves largely on him to "keep the peace" among the various divisions, each of which is seeking to protect and enlarge its domain. The CEO must constantly attempt to lower the level of overt or potential conflict, to achieve the basic cooperation that is essential to the well-being of the corporation.

Finally, the CEO must be the principal diagnostic strategist of the corporation. He must understand the true economic position of the company and have a vision about how to improve its performance over time. He must also define the path that the corporation must pursue toward its desired goals and assure that resources and risks are managed in such a way as to achieve them. In our view, the compulsions of the present are so great that most CEOs neglect, to a greater or lesser extent, the most critical of their responsibilities. A staff unit entitled "strategic planning" is no substitute for the CEO's continuing direct and personal involvement in strategic decision making.

In short, the allocation of money and people—the critical resources for the corporation's future gowth and profitability—is the CEO's major task. Since the amount of money and the number of able managers are never sufficient to permit even a large corporation to follow up on all the opportunities that it confronts, the critical task of the CEO is to pursue a resource allocation policy that holds the greatest promise for future success within a strategy of defined risk. If he has developed a cadre of senior managers with business acumen, the probability is greater that his long-run strategy will succeed.

9

Human Resources Agenda

We have advanced two major arguments. The first contends that the modern corporation has evolved structures that are dysfunctional for utilizing the abilities of its managerial personnel. The second stresses that these structures impede the CEO from effectively discharging his multiple duties, which include oversight of the corporation's human resources.

We have also explicitly raised and resolved an apparent paradox. That is, we have shown how our observations can be reconciled with the substantial and continuing profitability and growth of many large U.S. corporations. In brief, the early postwar years were characterized by highly favorable external circumstances and by a remarkably good alignment between what the large corporation was able to offer and what its young managers sought. To oversimplify, we can say that the young managers were in the right place at the right time. They wanted what many large corporations were able to provide.

But, as we have seen, the passage of time has changed that. The second large group of post–World War II entrants into the human resources pool, those who came of working age in the 1960s, had an orientation and value structure that was less well aligned with the corporate world. Moreover, many corporations were no longer able to treat the newest cohort as well as they had treated its predecessor, many of whom had enjoyed rapid salary increases, speedy promotions, and an opportunity to make a lot of decisions on their own.

Moreover, the new entrants exhibited a number of different characteristics from those of the previous cohort. A higher proportion had acquired more educational preparation. Many were MBAs or had earned a master's degree or doctorate in engineering or in one of the sciences. Individuals with such considerable general or specialized education look forward to using what they have learned and expect appropriate career opportunities and rewards.

As the campus rebellions in the late 1960s demonstrated, the new cohort of young people had less respect for authority in all sectors of life, including business leaders. And since these young people had grown up in affluent times, they assumed that the high levels of employment and gains in real income to which they had grown accustomed would continue. They placed less value than their predecessors on the promise of a lifetime career. As many opinion surveys have noted, the younger generation are more interested in the here-and-now, in the scope and freedom they have to shape and reshape their lives and careers. They see little point in putting up indefinitely with disagreeable elements in their jobs and careers in order to enjoy substantial benefits when they retire.

At the same time that the new managerial cohort is entering their corporate careers with expectations and values that are more difficult to realize, most large companies have been confronted by a constrained business environment that has resulted in fewer opportunities for managers to advance, less scope to raise managerial earnings and bonuses, and a reduced investment in their education and training. As profits began to slip, particularly in the recession of 1979–1983, top management found it necessary to close plants, encourage managers to take early retirement, and occasionally even resort to reductions in force. These actions undermined a key element of the corporate employment contract, namely, the implicit promise of a lifetime career.

The pervasiveness of such moves becomes clear when a successful company like IBM stresses in its 1983 annual report that "in those areas where the corporation has excess skills, incentives were offered to employees with 25 years or more of service to leave the company voluntarily." And their effects on managers are made equally clear in the following quote from the *Wall Street Journal* (April 19, 1984): "These are tense and confusing days for Getty's 19,400 world-wide employees, many of whom will be out of a job after years of steady employment. . . . The atmosphere around here is downright morbid."

Reduced or no profits meant that money and stock bonuses were temporarily cut or eliminated. Since these nonsalary emoluments are often a significant part of the total rewards of higher management, the losses to individuals were large. A classic instance of the adverse effects of the environment on executive compensation involved the CEO of International Harvester, Archie McCardell, in 1982. The provisions in his contract were such that the longer he stayed in his position, the greater were his losses.

Under these changed circumstances, the serious managerial dysfunction becomes more apparent. It stems, ultimately, from a combination of factors that trace back to scale, organizational structures that evolved as responses to scale, internal accounting systems that encourage political negotiations, and the receding of the market as a testing ground of an individual manager's business performance.

The extent to which these sources of dysfunction are linked to corporate size and complexity can be better understood if we contrast the large corporation with the small business enterprise.

Human Resources Agenda

In a small business enterprise, there is little diffusion of power: the owner-manager has it all, unless he chooses to delegate some to his immediate associates, with whom he remains in constant contact. A small enterprise has no need for an elaborate MIS; a simple system of accounts usually suffices. As to market tests, the small enterprise is overexposed. It must buy cheap, produce what customers will buy, and keep its prices competitive. It cannot afford to get out of alignment with the market on any of these fronts.

The managerial group in a small business is constantly responding to the market. The owner-manager always knows whether his associates in charge of procurement, manufacturing, and sales are doing better or worse than his competitors. And when it comes to assessing and rewarding them, he has no need to engage in an elaborate exercise. He knows from daily experience the strengths and weaknesses of his managers.

It would make little sense, however, to bemoan the loss of simplicity and the closeness to the market that characterize most small businesses. After all, small and medium-sized enterprises that are led by able men strive to become large enterprises, undeterred by the new difficulties that size and complexity bring in their wake. The lure of growth rests on potential gains inherent in size, scale, and synergy. Higher profits are made possible by economies in procurement, manufacturing, and marketing, together with financial resources to support long-term investments.

The outstanding characteristic of small business is its need to keep responding to market signals quickly and correctly. This crucial aspect of business often tends to be lost in the large corporation. Managers in large corporations engage in three different markets. The first is the external competitive market, in which goods are bought and sold. The second is the internal market, in which managers negotiate constantly with peers and with superiors to obtain the authority and resources they require to meet their targets and goals. And, finally, there is the long-term investment market, which is the primary responsibility of the senior managers, who must decide how to allocate those earnings that are not distributed to stockholders.

The number of extant large corporations attests to the fact that size, scale, and synergy are powerful contributors to the economies and efficiencies that result in corporate growth and profits. However, diseconomies are part of the same process of organizational growth and complexity. The diseconomies reflect the growing costs of coordination and the attendant losses in managerial effectiveness.

The large corporation therefore confronts a paradox. Through increasing scale and diversity it is able to achieve notable economies of scale, as outlined above. But in the process of achieving these economies it is forced to modify its organizational structure and decision-making mechanisms in ways that adversely affect the utilization of its managerial personnel.

Six Initiatives for Organizational Restructuring

From our statement of the problem it follows that in order to improve the climate for management performance, it will be necessary to change the corporate environment. We can single out three primary goals for changes, each related to one of the corporation's three markets. The first is to reposition managers so that they are more exposed to the marketplace and therefore able to be more responsive to its signals. The second goal is to reduce, as far as possible, the time and effort that managers devote to negotiating within the corporation for needed authority and resources. The third, and final, goal is to develop a long-term investment strategy that repositions corporate investments out of fields where the growth has leveled off or has begun to decline.

Through what actions can the large corporation move toward these goals? We suggest six initiatives.

192

Human Resources Agenda

First, the large corporation should reorganize itself so that its basic lines of business come as close as possible to being free-standing enterprises. In each of these basic businesses, the responsible managers should be in control of the authority and resources necessary to produce the business results for which they are held accountable. Each business entity should be relieved, as far as possible, of having to negotiate with other corporate units for approvals, resources, and support. Only in this way can clear-cut responsibility and accountability for performance be established and maintained.

Admittedly, the foregoing represents the desirable, not necessarily the feasible. In many instances a corporation cannot align its divisions completely with discrete products and distinct markets. The challenge that every CEO faces, however, is to decide on the number of different businesses he wants to be in and at the same time avoid proliferation and organizational complexity. This criterion surely underlies the recent accelerated movement to divestitures.

If senior and middle managers cannot be held accountable for their business goals, there is little or no prospect of the corporation's continuing to make money over the long pull. In the final analysis, only competent managers can make money. If the organization interferes with manager's ability to perform, the structure and decision-making mechanisms should be changed.

An alert corporation will also reduce the amount of time and effort that managers spend negotiating the charges levied against them by the MIS for the use of companywide services. The individual manager should determine how many, how much, and what quantity of these services his division requires. He is in the best position to make the necessary business tradeoffs. The emphasis on achieving major economies of scale through sharing large centralized services must be balanced off against the substantial costs of deflecting so much of line managers' energies into internal negotiations.

Currently, a line manager decides that he has more to gain by convincing the MIS group to change the charges levied against him rather than by directing his efforts to improved market performance by cutting real costs and increasing real revenues. Instead of continuing to seek significant economies from the use of common services, top management should be guided by a new assumption—that line managers can make significant gains for the corporation only by devoting more time to the market, less to internal negotiations. Corporate leadership, in effect, must seek to narrow the internal market by enlarging its line managers' scope for decision making.

Second, the MIS should be made more congruent with the financial accounts, as these come much closer to reflecting the true contribution of each business to the corporation's profits. In most large corporations, this will be difficult because of the many inconsistencies between MIS and financial accounting. But the need for reconciliation remains. Accountability in financial terms is the only broadly acceptable criterion for measuring business results. And it should be relied on in measuring and evaluating the performance of managers. All alternative methods contain too many arbitrary or imputed figures and therefore may provide false cues for behavior and decision making. Although financial accounting, too, has its limitations in correctly revealing the true contribution of each division, it is much less likely to result in gross distortions.

Third, managerial assignments should be restructed so that they are, wherever possible, linked to business performance. Assignments that principally involve "coordinating" and "control" functions should be drastically reduced and wherever feasible eliminated. Coordinating assignments cannot be entirely eliminated, of course, but whenever they make up a low proportion of the total number of managerial positions, we have one rough measure of organizational efficiency. Not only do these jobs often fail to contribute directly to business objectives, but they have the further disadvantage of stimulating the growth of corporate bureaucracy and the dysfunctional behavior it brings in its wake; and the larger the bureaucracy, the more room there is for "subjective" elements to dominate the performance appraisal system.

Fourth, the performance appraisal system should be reformed so that the key criteria have as much business content as possible and reflect business performance as accurately as possible. In turn, these performance elements should be measured statistically, with much less emphasis on supervisors' subjective judgments, which currently tend to contaminate the measurement system. The president of Intel, Andrew Grove, has stressed two points in his recent book (*High Output Management,* 1983): corporate performance is mostly the result of team performance, and effective performance appraisals are the key to good management. Regrettably he fails to link the two operationally, although he suggests how teamwork can be improved and how performance appraisals can be strengthened.

Fifth, more constructive use should be made of the compensation system, through greater reliance on incentives linked to real business results. The compensation structure in today's large corporation tends to reward team players. It tends also to reinforce a loose concept of "equity," in which all persons on the same level are treated more or less alike, with little regard for their differential contributions. Top management, in other words, tries to reduce discontent by not differentiating among managers unless there is hard evidence about their performance. But the real solution lies in reorganizing assignments and methods of evaluation so that managers' compensation can reflect their true contributions. Their work must be more closely linked to, and more directly measured in terms of, business outcomes.

The eight pages (95–103) that Robert Townsend devotes in his book (*Further Up the Organization,* 1984) to incentive compensation and profit sharing call attention to most of the critical issues. Townsend emphasizes—in our opinion correctly—the importance of building the system on performance: "[Remember that] incentive compensation is to measure variations in performance. The board should make a moral binder to devote 15 percent of pre-tax profits in perpetuity. Rate employees in one of three categories—unsatisfactory (no bonus), satisfactory (X), outstanding with the latter equal to 2X or greater. Keeping it simple means fighting the experts. Same problem with changing the rules or the percentages. Every change means loss of understanding, loss of trust, loss of motivation."

An article on "Rewarding Executives for Taking the Long View" (*Business Week,* April 2, 1984) reports on some potentially important changes introduced by Sears, Combustion Engineering, Borden, and a few other companies. These changes aim at tying executive compensation more closely to the real return on equity, not to more conventional but faulty measures of successful performance such as growth in sales. The articles goes on to observe, "Despite the apparent success of pay-for-performance ... the vast majority of companies which are talking about following suit are doing just that; still talking."

Sixth, top management must focus on strategic priorities, which largely determine the long-term success of the corporation. In other words, the CEO and his senior associates need to devote their primary attention to assessing the changing marketplace so that the decisions they make will help assure the corporation's future growth. To this end they must effectively allocate their key resources—people and money.

It was noted earlier that one of the great advantages of large firms is their ability to make sizable investments to improve their long-run position. These may take a number of forms: investments in state-of-the-art plants, expansion of existing or acquisition of new businesses that facilitate forward or backward integration, strengthening R&D efforts, and enhancement of human resources. But no corporation, even the largest, has sufficient resources at its command to move simultaneously along each of these axes. Priority setting is a must.

Economists call long-term investments "lumpy"—which means that large sums must be committed whenever a decision is taken to pursue one of the aforementioned strategies. Once made, a lumpy investment cannot readily be unmade, at least not without potentially large writeoffs.

It is important that top management assess its alternative investment plans in terms of financial data that reflect current capital costs and that it be conservative in estimating future profits. A prudent management is unlikely to be led astray by its calculations. But no matter how sound the underlying data and analyses, uncertainty will always be present. The capacity of senior managers to lead will be reflected in how often the future validates their judgments with respect to the factors that defied measurement, the elements of uncertainty.

A special report in *Business Week* (February 6, 1984) revealed that the stockholders of public companies that were acquired in 1979–1982 received a premium of just under 50 percent on the market price of their stock. Reformulated, this means that the executives of many acquiring companies had set themselves up for prospective failures which, as we know from a spate of recent divestitures, were not long in coming.

The time that top management takes to appraise an investment proposal and the amount of risk that it is willing to incur are central elements in its decision process. Even a well-positioned corporation with large capital resources cannot respond positively to all the reasonable requests for additional capital resources from all of its divisions.

Investments are necessarily speculative; their success depends on the fit between current assumptions and future reality. Since line managers generally know more about their particular businesses than the members of senior management, they are well positioned to plead their case. And since there are not sufficient funds to satisfy all requests, the decision-making group at the top must choose among them. One consideration in its decisions will be its estimate of the direction in which the macro economy and the specific industry are moving. Another is its assessment of the relative strengths of the competing claimants. Finally, the decision makers must distinguish between the merits of proposals and the persuasiveness of the data and the logic that undergirds them. Such discrimination is not easy since uncertainty is the essence of the case and the aim of each protagonist is to minimize the weight of unfavorable evidence.

If the competing divisions have incorporated the key business elements into their investment proposals and if top management has introduced the larger perspective of possible changes in the industry and economy, the basis for a reasonable decision has been established. This does not mean that the decision made will turn out to be right; it merely implies that the bases for the decision were sensibly developed and sensibly appraised.

The large amounts of money that must be committed to pursue a particular strategy and the difficulties of assessing the multiple uncertainties in an increasingly volatile economy have led an increasing number of top managements to search for solutions that appear to limit their risks. Thus senior managers may request yet another study in the hope that more data and more analysis will firm up some of the unknown factors. Or they may explore alternatives to making a lumpy investment. For example, by authorizing additional expenditures for advertising and marketing, they may generate more sales and more revenues in the short run, thereby obviating the immediate need for a new plant.

Even a large corporation cannot protect itself against the uncertainties in the market. But loss of nerve with regard to long-term investments may well lead to the worst of all possible responses.

To summarize, we believe that the following changes are needed:

- The large corporation should move as far as possible to organize its major businesses into essentially freestanding enterprises, with general managers who exercise substantial control over their resources.
- The scope of and need for negotiations in the internal

market should be reduced as much as possible.
- Primary reliance for assessing results should be placed on a system of financial accounting rather than on the MIS with its many artificial figures.
- Managerial assignments should be restructured so that fewer managers are involved in coordinating and controlling and more are responsible for revenue generation.
- Compensation should not be structured to treat managers equally; more emphasis should be placed on differential rewards based on performance.
- Senior management should focus more attention and energy on improving the long-term strategic position of the enterprise.

These basic initiatives will remove many current organizational barriers to the more effective use of management talent. But this is not the end of the story. Once the organization has been realigned, additional gains can be achieved by strengthening its human resources policies.

Human Resources Policy: Problems and Proposals

Beginning in the early 1950s successive groups of managers participating in the Columbia Graduate School of Business Executive Development Program at Arden House were asked if their company had a human resources division at the top of the organization with a vice-president in charge. Early on, only a few managers raised their hands, and then only tentatively because, as emerged when the issue was opened up for discussion, they were uncertain whether the CEO and his senior associates considered the human resources function important. A decade later, a fair number of the attendees reported that the personnel or human resources function in their company had been moved higher on the organizational chart. But they also noted that the senior executive in charge of personnel was not on a par with his colleagues in procurement, finance, marketing, and other long-established functions. Questioning brought out several continuing sources of weakness. First and foremost, most CEOs did not view the personnel function as critical and gave no evidence of real commitment to or leadership in this arena. Many CEOs had begun to refer to the importance of human resources in their speech-making, but beyond that they did relatively little other than to occasionally participate in an internal executive development seminar.

The roots of the problem lie, of course, in scale. As the organization increases in size and organizational complexity, the CEO becomes more distant from the middle managers. In today's large corporation, many managers with a decade or more service have never so much as laid eyes on the CEO. And even CEOs who are interested and willing to more actively oversee the human resources function know few of their middle managers since they generally respect the principle of the divisions' responsibility for hiring, developing, and assigning their managers.

In most large corporations, the senior human resources official finds it relatively easy to acquire an educational and training budget to provide new and enlarged opportunities for junior and middle managers. He is also likely to have a relatively free hand in modifying a wide range of personnel policies and procedures, from recruitment to pensions, subject only to the approval of his financial colleagues.

The more subtle aspects of his assignment, however, require that his colleagues at or close to the top be responsive to the human resources element and weigh it appropriately in their decisions, from acquisitions to plant location to divestitures. The script for agreement and action along these lines has not yet been written. Each senior human resources official must find his own way along this path, which necessitates major changes in the thought and behavior patterns of the CEO and the senior managers.

One of the more difficult challenges that large corporations face is to balance the short-term objectives of its various divisions with the long-term corporate goal of developing a group of experienced general managers. The accomplishment of the latter requires that divisions release some of their best people for reassignment, often at times when they feel that they cannot be spared. But unless a management development plan is in place and has strong support at the top, the corporation will sooner or later face significant deficits in its senior ranks.

The conventional practice in large corporations of finding employees who best match an "ideal type" is basically faulty. The concept of an ideal type is at variance with the characteristics of people who are being recruited as well as with research on life-cycle development; there are no reliable early indicators of future successful business behavior. And we cannot ignore the fact that a third and often a half of all recruits leave or are forced out by the end of five years. Perhaps the theory of the match fails because there is inadequate corporate experience to guide the selection process; or the experiences that an individual undergoes after joining the corporation may be so determining that initial perceptions are unimportant in influencing the stay-or-leave decision. Possibly, both explanations are valid.

There are further reasons to reconsider and change the established recruitment process. As noted earlier, the pool of college graduates with advanced degrees has been changing in terms of numbers, composition—many more women and more minorities—and general expectations, values, and goals. Even if the "ideal type" approach had some validity in the past, any effort to use it in the present and the future will almost certainly be counterproductive.

The high turnover among new recruits should be placed in the context of an earlier observation that a trainee's experiences are largely determined by the unit he joins and by his interactions with other individuals. Thus corporations need to pay more attention to the initial assignments of recruits and, especially, to their initial supervisors. Many years ago, the U.S. Army learned that its loss rate among new recruits during their first three months in the service was many times that of the British. Inquiry disclosed significant differences in the handling of recruits. The U.S. approach accentuated the sharp break between civilian and military life, in order to speed the process of adjustment to the military. But many new recruits were unable to cope with this abrupt transition. The British followed a more relaxed approach, smoothing the transition by assigning carefully selected noncommissioned officers to oversee the new recruits. The "mothering" sergeants took pride in salvaging the timid, the frightened, and the disoriented.

Since so much of a new employee's view of the corporation is determined by his early experiences, some attention to the orientation and support that new employees receive from their initial supervisors can make the difference between success and failure. Many middle managers have little interest in or aptitude for helping a young person to fit in. Others find the task a challenge and would welcome the opportunity to play a larger role, especially if their successful efforts were noted in their performance appraisals.

Every large organization must rely on routines in dealing with people. This is especially true when there are large numbers of undifferentiated individuals, such as new trainees and junior managers who have not had an opportunity to demonstrate the range of their capabilities. The problem of numbers, reinforced by the corporation's desire to proceed equitably, assures that the "system" quickly takes over. Newcomers are all too often assigned with little consideration of their personal preferences. A system that is insensitive to the individual concerns of the new employees sets the stage for negative experiences, which will be followed by high turnover.

Human Resources Agenda

As soon as possible, newcomers, as well as junior and middle managers, should have opportunities to make their career preferences known. The reason for this is simple: individuals who participate in decisions that affect them have a greater sense of responsibility and more incentive to achieve. Moreover, individuals surely know more than any personnel inventory possibly could about their own strengths, interests, and desires. And they are better positioned to factor in personal or family considerations that should be taken into account in deciding their assignments or reassignments. For example, because of past experiences or future expectations, they may prefer one work location to another. And if a new opportunity opens up, some persons would welcome being placed in a position with more responsibility and more risk, while others would prefer to avoid the challenge. The more the corporation can learn about how people see themselves and whether they are willing to bet on themselves, the better. Unless junior managers are asked and their answers are taken into account, many decisions taken by the personnel system will have unfavorable outcomes.

We called attention earlier to problems with the performance appraisal system that stem from its excessive reliance on subjective rather than business measures. There are other drawbacks as well. First, people are almost always rated "average" or "good." Most supervisors are disinclined to mark an employee "unsatisfactory" because to do so may set in motion procedures during which the supervisor will have to justify his appraisal. And supervisors also tend not to give "superior" ratings, for example, because they themselves are insecure or because they object to some facet of the employee's behavior that is only tangentially related to the effectiveness with which he carries out his assignments. The reasons that performance ratings are likely to be skewed in one or another direction are infinite, but they are almost always related to the politicized nature of the large corporation and to a lack of information about the employee's direct business contribution.

Second, the assessment of middle and higher managers is often confounded by the inability of the performance appraisal system to distinguish between short- and long-term criteria of successful performance. Many years ago, DuPont discovered that in its highly decentralized departmental system, managers were skimping on allocations for R&D because in the few years within which they had to be chosen for advancement to the executive committee (the top assignment), the benefits from such investments would not be reflected in their bottom line. Their successors might reap the rewards but not they. To circumvent this narrow managerial outlook, DuPont established a company-wide R&D division responsible for seeing that the departments made adequate investments.

Often higher management fails to include in its performance criteria results that contribute to the long-term strength of the corporation. Needless to say, among the factors that are often neglected is managers' effectiveness in dealing with their human resources. The life of a subsidiary manager is difficult enough without his having to pay attention to activities on which he is not measured. It is therefore imperative that his superiors include an assessment of how well he deals with his human resources (in terms of the number of his subordinates who become eligible for promotion, levels of turnover, reductions in head count, and any other measures that speak to the effectiveness with which he uses and adds to the competences of those under his control). In the early 1950s, the United States Army, recognizing the inadequacy of its officer evaluation system, modified it to include a number of points (unfortunately, not very many) that reflected the officer's human resources management capabilities.

Another problematic facet of corporate human resources policy, especially as it impacts on managerial personnel, is its preoccupation with time constraints on employees, expressed in required work hours. But the direct linkage of time to productivity is erroneous. Although most managers need ready access to their superiors, peers, and subordinates, such access requires an overlap of much less than the entire working day, as flex-time has demonstrated. Americans in particular tend to confuse busywork with accomplishment. We seem to believe that there is some special virtue to being busy all of the time, and we often ignore the question of whether the work being done contributes to the desired result.

Although the large corporation is making increasing use of a wide array of specialists, from research scientists to macroeconomists, its concept of work time is still a narrow one. Admittedly, many managers are permitted, even encouraged, to attend professional and trade association meetings and to enroll in and pursue specialized courses that add to their skills. Some are granted permission to make arrangements with neighboring universities, where they may teach a course, sometimes on company time. But such arrangements usually have to be individually negotiated among the manager, his supervisor, and the human resources staff.

It is difficult for a manager to achieve substantial control over the distribution of his time as well as freedom to determine how best to use it. Most large corporations simply do not believe that they can set objective targets for their managers and then leave it to the managers to use their time wisely. Yet only by doing so can they hope to elicit maximum motivation and productivity from today's more educated work force. Professionals want to exercise control over themselves, including their time, and are willing to be held accountable for their performance. The recent biography of André Mayer tells of his uncontrolled outbursts when he was unable to reach the CEO of Avis in mid-morning. Robert Townsend saw little point in hanging around the office once he had taken care of the pending issues, especially since he was far ahead of his goals and budget.

Large corporations have various justifications for their cautionary stances and tight controls over managers' time and work patterns. Some years ago a major chemical company turned down the request of some of its technical staff to open its laboratories on weekends and holidays on the ground that its insurance rates would be raised.

Ultimately, most large corporations believe that they are better off if their control over critical resources is tight, and this position carries over to their "ownership" of people. But talented and productive managers are less likely to remain in an employment relationship in which somebody else has major control over them, their opportunities to pursue career aspirations, what they work on, how they work, where they work, and so forth. There may be no easy answers to this issue of time and control, but surely it warrants more attention and experimentation than it has received. There has been some discussion and even some action regarding leaves of absence for selected professionals. But the range of possibilities is much greater and involves more substantial modifications. In particular, corporate employers must recognize the desire of professionally educated and trained persons to exercise optimal control over their time, patterns of work, and career configurations.

The increasing role that many large U.S. corporations are playing in the world market has led to another challenge to human resources policy. Most large enterprises now recognize that it is costly and otherwise dysfunctional to have the higher echelons of major overseas branches and subsidiaries staffed exclusively or even primarily with U.S. expatriots. Hence they have moved to fill as many of these positions as possible with local citizens. While this adaptation is sensible and reduces costs, it is not totally responsive to the underlying issues.

Those who move to the top of a major overseas division frequently have no place further to go. They are seldom assigned to a senior position in the United States, and without such reassignment they cannot compete for the top positions in the corporation. One can point to exceptions but they are just that— rare occurrences.

A related problem warrants attention. Since for many corporations, overseas sales account for between a third and a half or

Human Resources Agenda

even more of their annual revenue and profit and since policy is to use foreign nationals to staff overseas operations, senior U.S. management often knows far less than it should about the pull and push of forces abroad. The occasional trip by senior officials to key installations abroad—travel that often is linked to vacationing—is not adequate to provide the intelligence and know-how that senior management at home requires to respond to situations or to initiate actions.

A large business today is a global business, and its successful management requires working knowledge of the overseas market. Transnational assignments are essential to develop managers who can later become part of the effective transnational management group that is needed if the large corporation is to function effectively in the world's markets.

But most companies are not truly multinational. For example, consider the view of the CEO of Schlumberger: "We keep saying that Schlumberger is a multinational company. That is not true. We are a combination of Frenchmen and Americans. Not a bad combination. But fundamentally, in the 1980s we cannot ignore the rest of the world and the Pacific Ocean" (Auletta, *The Art of Corporate Success,* 1984, p. 74). Probably the company that comes closest to being a true multinational corporation is Royal Dutch/Shell.

Selective assignments for overseas duty of promising middle managers can provide a partial solution. Selective permanent assignments to corporate headquarters of foreign managers with a strong track record is another. Additional adaptations are worth considering. The one certainty is that top management cannot continue to ignore the issue.

The large U.S. corporation is now aware that it must reappraise a very basic and long-standing human resources policy. The corporation had always made the implicit commitment, in hiring a young management trainee, to provide, subject to satisfactory performance on his part, a lifetime career with opportunities for advancement all the way to the top. In earlier decades of rapid growth and high profitability, the large corporation had relatively little difficulty in fulfilling this commitment to the mutual satisfaction of both parties. But the volatility and uncertainty of today's business environment make this implicit understanding questionable.

The increased portability of private pensions and the greater importance that many successful managers now attach to challenging work make the implicit guarantee of lifetime employment—which experience has demonstrated is increasingly subject to being breached—lose much of its allure.

In any case, alternatives to lifetime employment carry their own problems and difficulties. Early and substantial vesting of benefits can speed the exit of able middle managers who have lost their first wind and who believe, often incorrectly, that they are blocked from further advancement. Consequently, the corporation may be left with a disproportionate number of managers who place a high value on employment security, which is all too often associated with mediocre performance. Moreover, as we know from the well-publicized cases of Polaroid and Kodak, a corporation that moves to speed early retirement can frequently experience a disproportionate loss of its more able managers. Further complications arise because of recent legislation that has reduced the margin of safety available to corporations seeking to thin their rolls of managers who are in the upper age brackets but still below sixty-five or seventy. If they are released without cause, these older employees may bring and win class action suits based on age discrimination.

It is relatively easy to recognize that an employment arrangement based on a career for life may no longer be optimal for either party—if, in fact, it ever was. What is far more difficult is to design alternative arrangements that will yield a higher level of mutual satisfaction and good performance. Accordingly the corporation should move away from the past practice of a broad commitment to a lifetime career for all who pass the probationary period.

Human Resources Agenda

It is ironic to note that just as the Japanese are taking the first steps to loosen the lifetime bond between corporations and their employees, many of our self-styled experts are recommending that we follow the traditional Japanese pattern. These experts are evidently unaware that the lifetime bond has been in force in many large U.S. corporations since the 1920s and in most since 1945.

To assure that they are better able to develop and effectively utilize their managerial talent, large corporations must undertake the following actions:

- A senior corporate executive with responsibility for the human resources function should be established on a par with the other senior executives and should have a role in all important decisions involving the use of the corporation's personnel.
- The corporation must have in place a management development system that requires the divisions to release key personnel for new assignments in order to broaden and deepen their experiences and competences as they move toward the top.
- The approach of recruiting an "ideal type" should be abandoned because of excessive turnover among recruits and the availability of new sources of supply.
- More consideration should be given to the initial assignments of recruits, and supervisors who can aid in the process of their corporate assimilation should be identified and rewarded.
- As early and as much as possible, junior managers should be consulted about their next work assignments, since this consultation will result in a greater engagement on their part.
- The major failings of extant performance appraisal systems should be recognized and efforts made to modify them in

the direction of greater reliance on objectively measurable business results.

- The tight controls exercised over the time that managers spend in the office are increasingly inappropriate—particularly for professionals whose performance cannot be assessed in terms of the hours that they spend on the job—and should be modified.
- Large U.S. corporations operating worldwide should explore ways of providing their ablest foreign managers with an opportunity to compete for senior positions.
- Since large corporations need to retain optimal flexibility in the use of their managerial personnel, they should explore alternatives to their traditional practice of lifetime employment.

The foregoing recommendations, together with the earlier ones that addressed organizational restructuring, indicate the directions the large corporation can take to better align its structure to the needs and preferences of its managers. It would be presumptuous to claim that if these fifteen recommendations were implemented, they would assure that large corporations could continue to grow and be profitable. We do believe, however, that the directions suggested by our agenda will reduce some, probably many, of the difficulties that large corporations are encountering in making effective use of their managerial personnel.

PART IV

Resolutions

10

The Uncertain
Future

In assessing the future of the large corporation, we must place it within the dynamic U.S. economy, which is increasingly weighted in favor of industries based on new knowledge and new technologies. These industries are characterized more than ever by the high caliber and productive use of their human resources. In a steel plant, managerial and technical personnel account for about one of every twelve workers; in an advanced electronics establishment, college-educated personnel account for more than two of every five members of the work force. The discovery and application of new knowledge is the key to maintaining economic growth and prosperity.

More generally, the U.S. economy, like all advanced economies, is dominated by the activities of large enterprises operating across the spectrum of economic affairs. The large corporation is in fact the prototypical institution of the modern economy. In certain sectors, such as manufacturing, large corporations provide a high proportion of all jobs.

We have earlier described the changing dynamics of the

human resources pool in the United States and the massive investments that our society has made to improve the quality of its human resources. The impressive upgrading in educational achievement, the advances in health care, and in research and development have contributed significantly to raising the national level of human competence. This qualitative upgrading of the work force has created a labor pool with both better skills and higher expectations. We noted that today's manager is an educated individual who looks to his work as a principal medium for achieving personal fulfillment.

All employees, particularly those who go to work for a large corporation after a long period of education and training, bring with them into the workplace a set of personal values, knowledge, skills, and expectations. These better educated persons expect their work to provide them opportunities to become meaningfully involved in the affairs of their work unit and over time with the large corporation itself; they expect to enjoy career opportunities, with promotions and rewards based on performance.

During the many generations from the onset of modern industrial expansion following the Civil War until the election of Franklin Delano Roosevelt in 1932, the basic contract between employers and workers consisted of twelve, ten, and eventually eight hours a day on the job; supervisors had the power to hire (and fire) workers whose wages provided them with the necessities of life and little more. When Secretary of Labor Frances Perkins in 1933 sought to address the steel workers in Homestead, Pennsylvania, the only land in that city that was not owned by the U.S. Steel Corporation was the U.S. Post Office, the site of her speech.

The members of today's work force cannot be treated simply as hired hands; they cannot be told what to do and be expected to do it. Rather, they want to play a part in determining how they work and to have a voice in establishing the wages and benefits they receive, just as they expect to influence their own career progression; they also expect and insist that they will be considered for advancement and promotion in accordance with their seniority and competence. If they have made a substantial investment in themselves prior to entering the work force, they will attach more importance to their ability to guide their work and careers. The human resources "credo" of most large corporations emphasizes the commitment of top management to help their managers pursue their career goals and realize them. Large enterprises that are able to organize and maintain a work environment in which the reality approximates the credo will have greater success in making effective use of their people, which in turn should be reflected in the corporation's increasing the value of the enterprise for its stockholders. Top management faces the challenge of putting a "people first" priority into place.

In its *Annual Report–1983*, a generally upbeat account of its present and future prospects, RCA called special attention to its managerial personnel: "Increased emphasis has been placed on the identification of key management resources and succession planning for middle- and upper-management positions throughout the company. During 1983, more than 1,600 managers were promoted which represents about 15 percent of the total management group."

As we have observed, the managerial group is the most critical to long-term corporate growth and profitability. The managerial group is the repository of most of the operating experience and wisdom embedded in the enterprise. It runs the business, makes most of the decisions, and is essentially responsible for the "informal" organization—the way things really work. Management, in reality, is "the organization." The performance and productivity of the managerial group are the touchstones of the organization's performance in the marketplace.

Against this perspective, we have called attention to the major lines of development of large U.S. corporations, particularly in the post–World War II period. During this "golden age" of American business, the human resources climate in many large firms was good, more often by inadvertence than by design. In

216 a period of rapid growth, it was relatively easy for large U.S.

a period of rapid growth, it was relatively easy for large U.S. corporations to provide attractive opportunities for many of its managerial personnel. In a rapidly expanding business, new jobs and rapid promotions are the order of the day, salary levels tend to rise, and there are many opportunities for personal growth through successively more important career assignments.

But the golden age came to an end in the late 1960s and early 1970s, which saw the acceleration of inflation, the intensification of international competition, and other developments dysfunctional to continued prosperity and growth of the American economy. Moreover, matters took a turn for the worse inside the large U.S. corporation as a result of its organizational responses to its own growth and complexity.

Let us summarize our discussion of developments to date. During the quarter century after World War II, the large corporation continued to adhere basically to a hierarchical structure, in which managers on each succeeding level of the organization had control over those below them. Increasing scale and complexity, meanwhile, resulted in the delegation of considerable operating responsibilities to decentralized units, with a corresponding diffusion of power. There was a poor fit between the old and the new patterns of organization and decision making. Power remained centered at the top, and the increment distributed to the operating divisions was insufficient to give line managers the flexibility they needed. And although a primary purpose of this shift was to allow the CEO and his senior associates to focus on strategic matters, in point of fact they found most of their time and energy consumed in trying to keep the various divisions in some tolerably cooperative mode. There were a spate of negative consequences. The work climate worsened; many managers felt thwarted in their attempts to use their skills and potential; and more and more of top management's efforts had to be directed to coping with the rising frustrations and inefficiencies of its subordinates. Additional difficulties have arisen because many of the line managers to whom operating

The Uncertain Future

responsibility was delegated did not at the same time gain control over the critical resources they needed to carry out their charters. As a result, there occurred a misalignment of responsibility, targets, and resources so that accountability became impractical or impossible. Such malfunctioning leads inevitably to lower employee motivation and performance.

Today's large corporation, as we have seen, is highly politicized. Its managers are continually looking inward to catch any shift in the power constellation so that they can adjust to it before they find themselves on the losing side. They inevitably have less time and energy for the marketplace, the only arena where profits can be earned. As we noted earlier and here reemphasize, the accumulation of a cushion contributes to deflecting management's attention from the marketplace. A long period of good profits creates a sense of false security, which in turn leads to dysfunctional behavior.

The large corporation, as it is now organized, has only limited capacity to utilize its people effectively in their primary mission of adding economic value to the corporation. And the adverse environment also has direct negative effects on employees since it leads to experiences that are at variance with both their expectations and the firm's credo. As these dysfunctional aspects become more widespread, the corporation's future is at risk.

At some point the costs of internal coordination can come to exceed the gains from scale and synergy. More and more managers believe and act on the assumption that they have more to gain from focusing their energies on internal politics and the pursuit of power. In the face of the conditions discussed, effective leadership at the highest levels of the corporation becomes progressively more difficult to achieve and maintain. The conclusion is paradoxical: many large corporations, as they approach the apex of their dominance in the marketplace, are already weakened and vulnerable to decline because of the incipient erosion of the very strengths that sped their earlier growth and success.

The large corporation at risk moves along a familiar path. Growth in earnings and return on capital tend to moderate. Often the deceleration of the rate of profits conceals an accumulation of potential corporate deficits, which are permitted to remain hidden, at least for a time, by accounting conventions and/or regulatory procedures. The CEO, as the custodian of the firm's fortune and fate, is hampered by lack of information, corporate mores, and conflicting advice as he attempts to analyze the true situation and to take action to work off losses previously incurred but not recorded. The board of directors is seldom sufficiently knowledgeable or sufficiently independent to force corrective actions. Furthermore, a slow secular decline in a major arena is often misread as a cyclical phenomenon that time will cure. This misreading allows top management to procrastinate before taking corrective action. The large enterprise, hobbled by a rigid organizational structure and a slow-responding decision-making mechanism, finds it difficult to adjust to a volatile market. It also encounters problems in designing and executing successful acquisitions and divestitures. Relatively modest and diffuse R&D investments often fail to generate the momentum that could make a difference to the firm's overall performance. And few large corporations have been successful to date in managing venture businesses.

Some large corporations have sought to break out of their constrained mode by investing a part of their profits in new ventures. The enthusiastic supporters of this new approach emphasize the advantages that will flow from giving the entrepreneurial manager more authority and freeing him from having to beg or borrow resources as well as from the tight supervision of the corporate staff. Under such conditions, they argue, the new venture will have a chance to grow, mature, and become profitable. As yet, however, there are relatively few successful examples of this hybrid in organizational structure—the largely independent small venture unit within the large hierarchical behemoth. The emergent successes, such as IBM's personal computer operation, have attracted, as one might have expected, a great amount of favorable comment. Yet the last annual report of IBM (March 1984) made only modest claims for this organizational innovation, despite its optimism about the corporation's ability to dominate the low end of the market.

Burdened by the high costs of internal coordination and ineffective utilization of its human resources, the large enterprise is increasingly vulnerable to the entry of small and medium firms into its markets. Its vulnerability is usually in the specialized segments of these markets, where the small firm can be more attentive and responsive to selected customer groups. These new competitors, unburdened by massive prior investments and free of the heavy costs of internal coordination, are frequently able to offer superior products and thereby capture the small end of the market. The large-scale competitor must therefore focus increasingly on the upper end, where transaction size and gross profitability are still large enough to cover its costs. Over time, many large corporations must yield large segments of what had earlier been highly profitable markets to the new competition.

These shifts in market shares put increasing pressure on profit margins. If international competition intensifies, the erosion of profits is likely to accelerate. When a large firm loses its market dominance, it is in fundamental difficulty. Huge investments not written down to true market value are no longer producing profitable results, and management realizes that these locked-in investments cannot be recaptured without incurring large losses. At this stage the firm is on the brink of major trauma. It confronts large write-offs, is vulnerable to takeover bids, and may even have to file for bankruptcy. If the firm is in an essential industry, as are Lockheed and Chrysler, the federal government may provide assistance on the ground that the nation cannot risk the losses that would be entailed if the firm were allowed to fail.

As presently constituted, the large corporation usually finds it difficult to deal with problems of this order until it has reached the point where its very survival is at issue. At this stage, however, the surgery that is required may kill the patient. Massive discharges, plant closures, public subsidies aimed at buying time, or bankruptcy itself all indicate earlier failure to act. If disaster cannot be avoided, the remaining question is how society will distribute the burden of the ensuing losses. No matter what actions are taken by government and the firm's creditors, the employees inevitably bear a great part of the loss. Such an outcome represents the final blow to the expectations of the managers, who had expected to find personal growth and fulfillment in the workplace.

The fact that corporate growth often leads to conditions contributing to corporate demise has the quality of a Hegelian dialectic. Scale elicits a series of organizational responses that even talented business leaders may eventually not be able to control and manage effectively. When control is lost, the firm becomes vulnerable to buffeting by market forces, which further undermine it, until eventually it must shrink and reorganize, usually at great loss.

We can offer no definitive solutions to this overriding threat brought on through inflexibilities resulting from scale. A set of prescriptive initiatives aimed at making greater use of the corporation's human resources and thereby placing the large-scale enterprise on a more productive course was outlined in the previous chapter. We argued there in favor of organizing or reorganizing the firm into integrated core businesses, with responsibility, authority, and accountability placed on those business managers who had strong track records of profit making. We urged that debureaucratization of the corporation and a shift from reliance on a flawed internal MIS to reliance on financial accounting. Further, we recommended that the firm pay more attention to incentive compensation geared to the profit contribution of managers of the core businesses. We went on to point out that such redirections could be achieved only if there were

The Uncertain Future

a true delegation of operating responsibilities and if the CEO initiated further changes at the top of the organization. He and his senior associates would have to follow a policy of marking business assets at their true market values and disposing of, spinning out, or repositioning assets before major problems become embedded in the balance sheet.

The overall aim of such far-reaching initiatives is to create a climate of "business-mindedness" in the large corporation. In other words, the behavior of managers must be primarily geared to success in the marketplace over the long pull, in contrast to their current preoccupation with fighting their way up the corporate hierarchy through alliances and maneuvering.

We do not want to give the impression that the sort of redirection we have outlined is a matter simply of understanding and action on the part of the CEO and board of directors. The challenge is a difficult one. Before he can take even the first step, the CEO must understand that the organization in place, which has performed well in the past, has become flawed. Next, he must convince himself, his senior associates, and the board that the substantial risks and costs of restructuring the corporation are justified in terms of greater gains in the future. Finally, he must have the self-confidence, drive, and energy to proceed with what will be a difficult undertaking.

Many CEOs are aware, or are becoming aware, that the organizations they lead are poorly positioned to use their human resources effectively. And they are willing—in some cases, even eager—to introduce changes that they hope will contribute to better outcomes. But others are cautious, uneasy about sending signals to their stockholders or, if they move aggressively to restructure, afraid of engendering conflicts among their associates. These CEOs usually settle for marginal adjustments. But marginal adjustments frequently fail since they do not address the major sources of malfunctioning. As a result, many large corporations continue to operate at a suboptimal level until their mounting difficulties bring them face to face with a crisis they cannot possibly escape without undertaking drastic changes. And by that time they may have lost their capacity to maneuver.

Macroeconomic Parameters

As is true of all institutions, the large corporation operates within a societal framework. Leadership structures, the financial markets, the law, and macroeconomic policy set the boundaries within which the corporation must operate. And beyond these are the still more potent sociopolitical factors which will largely determine its future. In order to better assess the corporation's future we will take up each of these two sets of factors in turn.

The legal owners of a public corporation are its stockholders, whom the board of directors represents and on whose behalf it acts. Thus when we look at leadership structures, a question that immediately arises is whether the conventional board operates close to its optimum. In most cases, the answer is probably no, for a variety of reasons. Many boards are dominated by the CEO, there are too many inside directors (senior corporate managers), and boards are frequently supine when a CEO insists on staying beyond his retirement date.

Partial remedies lie at hand. Outside directors have a responsibility to play a more active role in filling vacancies on the board and in preventing the CEO from stacking the board with insiders who work for him. The board has an obligation to serve as a check and balance to the CEO and not become a rubber stamp. Never is such independence more important than when the CEO approaches the age of retirement. This is illustrated in Courtney C. Brown's recent book, *The Dean Means Business* (Columbia Graduate School of Business, 1984), which reports a number of horror stories about CEOs who simply would not leave at the previously agreed-upon time. Boards must also seek to restructure bonus payments for the CEO and other senior executives to reflect long-term rather than short-term performance.

Some have proposed that boards be reconstituted to include a number of "public directors." The idea is that such directors, with independent staff support, would be in a stronger position to protect the stockholders and advance the public interest. But the proposal never caught on, and it probably would not have worked if it had. It would have been difficult to identify suitable candidates willing to serve in such a role. Furthermore, new tensions would undoubtedly have developed among these public directors, the other directors, and the CEO.

A more modest and constrained set of suggestions for strengthening the role of boards of directors was advanced by a former business executive with extended experience as a board member. In an article in the *Harvard Business Review* (March–April 1984), he urged the elimination of post-retirement benefits and improper executive perks, an increase in directors' stock ownership, and a limitation on multiple directorships.

Most important, the board, at least its key members, must be more than tangentially involved in choosing the new CEO. It is right and proper for them to give weight to the recommendation of the retiring CEO, especially if he himself has been highly successful. But even in that circumstance the board has the obligation to assess the finalists. If board members do not participate actively in the final decision, this is tantamount to the nonfulfillment of their statutory responsibilities. In our litigious society, a future stockholders' suit cannot be ruled out.

Strengthening boards of directors along the lines we have suggested will not necessarily transform the large corporation. But it could add to its efficiency and, in the process, reassure investors that their interests will not be ignored by a self-perpetuating management.

Well-functioning financial markets are a sine qua non for a flourishing corporate environment. One of the principal responsibilities of top management is to protect and increase the assets of the company. In discharging these responsibilities, it may decide to sell off a mature business unit and buy a company in a field that holds more promise of expansion. Some may look on this buying and selling of companies as antithetical to industrial capitalism's basic purpose of producing at a competitive price more and better goods and services that the consumer needs or wants. But without acquisitions and divestitures top management could not protect and increase the assets over which it has stewardship.

Moreover, the proponents of the present system, with its elaborate and finely tuned capital markets, insist that the only effective discipline on management and the only true protection for stockholders come through the efficacy of the financial markets. They can point to many instances to support their case, the most recent and dramatic being the large gains that accrued to the stockholders of Gulf Oil as a result of the actions of Mr. Pickens and his associates.

Financial markets are the foundation on which our evolving corporate system rests. But that does not mean that all the buying and selling of companies that has been taking place in recent years necessarily strengthens the corporate balance sheet or increases stockholders' equity. Far from it.

During the late 1960s there was a wild rush to establish conglomerates, with Harold Geneen of ITT out in front and Charles Bluhdorn of Gulf & Western not far behind. More recently, however, a countermove has been gaining momentum. Many CEOs have decided that it is neither easy nor profitable to run a highly diversified company, no matter what portfolio principles they follow. Making money in competitive markets requires more than driving subordinates to meet their budget goals. The *Wall Street Journal* (May 25, 1984) carried a major story under the headline "R. J. Reynolds Turns to Lines It Knows Best." The story reported on how Reynolds is pulling out of petroleum and shipping and "preparing to make an even

The Uncertain Future

bigger splash in consumer products—businesses for which it is best known."

The recent rash of leveraged buy-outs, which has not yet run its course, is in essence the antithesis of the earlier move toward conglomeration. In a leveraged buy-out, investors bet on key managers who, having had experience in the business and the industry, can presumably run the company better, pay off the high debts that the buy-out assumed, and earn for themselves and for others a satisfactory premium. All this, then, will be achieved on the basis of superior management skills, which will have more scope now that managers are no longer constrained by the heavy hand of corporate bureaucracy. As the *Asset-Based Finance Journal* (Citicorp Industrial Credit, Inc.) reported in its Winter 1984 issue: "Five entrepreneur-minded executives of Gulf and Western Industries, Inc. joined together to form Conger Corporation which last March purchased Gulf and Western's domestic cigar business for $120 million." Alexander Brainard, who heads the new unit, commented: "The freedom is from paperwork, the layers and layers of vertical management, and the voluminous policies and procedures that of necessity characterize large corporations."

Business Week (April 30, 1984) had an article entitled "Bairnco: An Empire That Spins Off Companies to Grow." Chairman Glenn W. Bailey was quoted as saying "Big companies kill the entrepreneurial spirit. I'd much rather have five $200 million companies with highly motivated management than an institutionalized $1 billion one." As the article made clear, Bailey himself gives managers incentives, a free hand, and often a stake in the business.

Finally, well-functioning capital markets have played a significant role in stimulating the growth of new firms, particularly those in high tech. Once the federal government eliminated the tax discriminations against newly formed enterprises that were beginning to accumulate capital, the capital markets responded strongly. Essentially, the available capital plus a large pool of embryonic entrepreneurs and a large potential market eager for new products make for rapid economic growth. This conjunction of factors has been present in high tech, which has absorbed over 40 percent of all new investment in recent years. Access to venture capital funds, made possible by well-functioning capital markets, is thus essential for the continuing start-up of new firms, some small proportion of which will become the large corporations of tomorrow.

Antitrust remains a potent instrument of public policy. The divestiture of AT&T is a powerful reminder that even the world's largest corporation was not exempt from its rule. However, it is hard to say whether a particular corporate decision will or will not reduce competition. Not surprisingly, there are often differences of opinion among the interested parties—corporate executives, government officials, lawyers, and economists. In 1983–1984 the Department of Justice stood by and interposed no objection to major acquisitions in the oil industry but stepped in to prevent two major mergers in steel. Moreover, the Secretary of Commerce sharply disagreed with the Attorney General over the steel mergers. He felt that in the absence of such mergers, the American steel industry would become increasingly vulnerable to foreign competition and would eventually lose out in the U.S. market. After additional negotiation the LVT–Republic merger was approved. And shortly thereafter Nippon-Kokan gained approval to acquire a 50 percent interest in National Steel.

In fact, a growing number of informed persons, both in and out of government, have urged that the antitrust strategy be reassessed in light of the significantly different relations that exist in many other countries between government and key export industries and firms. The revisionists argue that unless our long-term approach is modified very soon, many U.S. corporations will find themselves unable to compete successfully against the many foreign firms that are aided, instead of hobbled, by their governments.

A number of antitrust constraints have been relaxed, and

competitors are now permitted to finance a common export strategy or major R&D projects. In the banking industry, earlier strict regulations at both the federal and state level have been relaxed.

These brief comments about antitrust and deregulation provide background to the amorphous debate that has been under way in recent years over whether the United States needs an "industrial policy." Government at every level—local, state, and federal—has, of course, always played a major role in shaping the economy, both by action and by inaction. On the positive side, we need only recall the dominant role of government in such critical sectors as transportation, forestry, agriculture, housing and land use, banking, public utilities, education, and health care. And, more generally, government has exercised a shaping influence on the economy through taxes, regulations affecting foreign trade, antitrust regulations, the control of credit, funding for research and development, and many other interventions.

In the current argument over industrial policy, advocates want to see established at the federal level a formal body that will systematically consider what government can do to strengthen the economy. Their opponents favor a continuation of ad hoc actions to meet emergencies, as in the Chrysler case.

The choice in this debate is by no means clear-cut. But until the pros spell out more specifically what they have in mind and how they plan to proceed, it is probably best to take a cautious stance on enlarging the responsibilities of the federal government for macro policy. Its record to date should serve as a reminder of its limitations as well as its potential for constructive intervention.

The Sociopolitical Environment

There are a number of sociopolitical and economic forces that will undoubtedly exercise a significant transforming influence on the large corporation. We will look briefly at several of these forces: internationalization, domestic politics, technology, education, and the changing value structure of the American citizen.

One of the foundations for the postwar growth of both the developed and developing nations was the intensification of their commercial and financial dealings with one another. During this period, internationalization expanded the profit-making opportunities of large U.S. corporations, through specialization and the extension of the market. More recently, however, internationalization has taken the form of intensified competition. Thus it has also increased the risks that U.S. corporations face. Looking to the future, it appears that internationalization will accelerate and that the volatility of the market will increase. These trends, in turn, will make additional demands on the capacity and the flexibility of large corporations to respond rapidly and decisively.

The future interactions between the large U.S. corporation and domestic politics are more difficult to discern. Since the Great Depression, the large U.S. corporation has for the most part escaped political debate. The environmental legislation of the 1970s was not punitive, and both Carter and Reagan were able to win some points by pressing for deregulation. Large-scale business enterprises have been the beneficiaries of the recent skepticism about the ability of government to perform effectively. The widespread presumption is that businesses are more efficient than public bureaucracies. There is periodic criticism, however, of occasional high-handed and improper business actions, from environmental damage to untruthful advertising.

It is difficult to know when, if ever, a powerful political leader such as Theodore Roosevelt may once again seek and win votes by attacking the large corporation. No major political leader since then has repeated his broad-scale attack on big business, and such an attack seems unlikely in the foreseeable future. We can cautiously conclude that in the absence of a serious and prolonged malfunctioning of the U.S. economy, the large corporation will remain relatively safe from political harassment. One caveat: if a number of large U.S. banks are jeopardized by the collapse of the international debt structure, and if their collapse has widespread domestic ramifications, this sanguine conclusion may not hold.

There has been much speculation about the impact of the new technology, particularly the microprocessor, on the future of the economy, including the large corporation. A wide range of scenarios have been constructed. Some writers suggest that a high proportion of all middle managers will become redundant and that most work will be carried out by persons sitting in front of terminals in their own homes.

A more cautious approach would anticipate that in selected industries a sizable reduction in the ranks of middle management will occur. Such a change is already under way in insurance, where agents in the field can directly access the corporate computer to ascertain current rates. In addition, computer-communications networking is sufficiently advanced to permit the movement of considerable back-office work out of the major urban centers to outlying communities. Several New York City-based firms have moved key operations to small cities in the Midwest and to the South.

One tantalizing question, to which we have no answer, is whether and how soon the further development of the microprocessor will enable relatively small freestanding manufacturing plants to compete successfully by achieving significant economies in batch operations that would enable them to respond more effectively to local markets. The small, highly computerized, specialized steel mill points to such a development. If such downscaling were to become pervasive, one of the foundations of the large manufacturing corporation's success—namely, economies of scale—would be permanently weakened.

Major changes have occurred in the human resources pool, mainly through the broadening and deepening of the educational system. Also important have been the significant shifts in values and expectations of the new entrants into the work force, which have critical consequences for the future structure and functioning of the large corporation.

A related trend has been the sizable public investments in research and development. Such investments increased from about 1 percent of GNP in 1950 to about 3 percent of a much larger GNP in the mid-1960s, before sliding back to their current level of around 2.5 percent. They unquestionably contributed to enlarging the pool of basic knowledge, as well as opening up and accelerating applications in a wide variety of fields: nuclear power, biomedicine and biogenetics, communications and space, electronics and computers, aerospace, pharmaceuticals, and still other fields in which the large U.S. corporation has been able to take and hold the lead.

As we look ahead a decade or two into the next century, which will coincide with the working life of the cohort that has recently entered the work force, we must realize that the ability of top management to meet its many challenges will depend on more than its ability to change its own structures, operations, and reward systems. Whether it succeeds in meeting its challenges will depend in no small measure on public policies and actions— especially those bearing on the educational establishment, including research and development. No large corporation is able to develop its human resources from scratch. That responsibility lies with the individual, the family, philanthropy, and government. Much the same holds for expanding basic knowledge. That depends in the first instance on the scale and scope of the federal R&D effort.

We see, then, that the large corporation can act on two fronts. It has considerable scope to affect the quality of its human resources through its own actions. And it can play a parallel role by helping to formulate public policy as to the level and direction of public investments aimed at expanding the pool of talented people available for work.

If we are indeed living in a world characterized by an

acceleration in the rate at which knowledge and techniques are becoming obsolescent, the large corporation must act to insure that its personnel keep up with the developments that occur over the years in their areas of specialization. Unless it takes positive action to avoid such obsolescence, the corporation will surely be at risk. Significantly, one of the leaders of American science and technology has remarked that in contrast to his repeated in-depth conversations with senior Japanese business leaders, he has never been able to engage in a broad-ranging technical discussion with an American CEO.

The large U.S. corporation, especially if it is in a science-based industry, must understand that it faces much the same challenge that institutions of higher education have confronted for many generations. It must insure that its personnel remain competent and up-to-date in their respective fields so that they will be able to oversee successive cohorts of newcomers and continue themselves to make productive contributions. We have no simple solutions to recommend but see several changes as prerequisites to constructive action. The large corporation should relax its tight control over the working schedules of many of its key managers, especially those with technical responsibilities. It should encourage these managers to pursue linkages with colleagues in academe and elsewhere and provide them with sabbaticals. And it should look with favor on nonexclusive employment contracts as long as proprietary knowledge is protected. More generally, the corporation should continue to experiment with a host of other approaches, many still to be designed.

Each of the four parameters that we have discussed—internationalization, domestic politics, technology, and education—has shown how the large corporation is significantly affected by ongoing changes in the macroenvironment. The same point can be made by looking at our fifth parameter—the alterations that are occurring in the value structures of the individual and the larger society. The direction of some of these changes can be discerned. For example, we can see how the family is being transformed as a result of values that lead to later marriages, more divorces, fewer children, and the pursuit of careers by both spouses. But the direction of many other changes, particularly those embedded in the evolution of the economy, remain to be revealed. No one knows, for example, whether we will sooner or later enter on another long sustained period of economic growth or, for that matter, whether the recent high levels of unemployment will recede to a tolerable level or remain at a midpoint where they will leave millions of able-bodied and industrious Americans with no regular attachment to the world of work.

And unless international relations, especially between the superpowers, take a distinct turn for the better, we may be on a downward slope that could lead to nuclear warfare. On the premise that the missiles will not be fired, the following suggests how the emerging value structures may affect the large corporation.

The young people who complete college and graduate or professional school are seeking a broad range of satisfactions from their work and careers. They want not only economic rewards and long-term material benefits but also opportunities to use their competences, to test themselves, to compete for advancement, to be judged on how they perform, and to add to their knowledge and skills. The extent to which they press to realize these goals will, of course, depend in no small measure on the extent to which the macroenvironment is favorable. But in any event, these and related values, which have been crystallizing for some time, are likely to become dominant in the decades ahead. It would be foolish for the large corporation to assume otherwise or to delay responding to them. The gaps between managerial expectations and corporate reality which we identified earlier are widening all the time, to the disadvantage of both parties.

The Uncertain Future

Although this book has centered on the managerial dimensions of the large corporation, we want to call attention to the fact that in a democratic society no large group—managers, scientists, farmers, blue-collar workers, women, minorities—will stand by passively and tolerate for long a policy of inaction if their crucial values and aspirations are ignored or denied. If a previously responsible institution fails, as did the competitive market in the 1929–1933 period, the citizenry will seek an alternative. The New Deal was just that. More recently, when the Cold War was at its height, President Eisenhower, although opposed to the involvement of the federal government in education, had no choice but to sign the National Defense Education Act. After the racial disturbances in metropolitan centers of the mid-1960s, President Johnson was able to persuade many captains of industry to change their recruitment and hiring in order to offer more jobs to unemployed blacks.

There is no need to add to these illustrations. If leaders of existing institutions have demonstrated that they are unable or unwilling to change their ways, a virile democracy will explore new approaches to accomplish its objectives. We are convinced that the large corporation is at risk because its working environment is no longer satisfactory to its work force. We have focused on its managerial personnel but the shortcomings involve all of its employees.

Many analysts believe that the economy is sound and that the leadership role of the large corporation is secure. Our assessment is more cautious. We are struck by the ambivalent testimony of history—the continued dominance of the large corporation as a genus but the disappearance of many large corporations along the way. We are also struck by the increasing volatility of the national and international economies, a characteristic that will surely make more difficult the survival and growth of large corporations.

But we are also impressed by the considerable flexibility and adaptability that large corporate enterprises have demonstrated in confronting and surmounting the challenges of new technology, war, accelerating inflation, periods of rapid economic growth as well as periods of deep depression, and still other major shocks.

We are reasonably certain, however, that the growing nonfit between the corporation's structure and its managerial personnel is a serious threat to the survival of the large corporation. It must be confronted. We do not know whether successful remedies can be developed, although we believe that they can. Nor do we know whether a large corporation that learns to make more effective use of its managerial talent will thereby assure its future. But we are certain that if it does not make the effort and succeed in realigning its structure to meet the needs of its people, it will be at risk.

INDEX

Index

Index

teria in, 171; growth and, 121–22, 127–33; impact of scale on, 133–36; internal reporting system in, 123–26; market behavior and, 10; and obstacles in responding to change, 136–40; Simon on, 65–66; top management in, 161–62

Defense, U.S. Department of, 36–38, 45, 90, 175

Defense Science Board, 37

Delegation, 19, 21, 217

Deregulation, 226–28

Diversification, 142; *see also* Acquisitions; Mergers

Divestitures, 14–15, 128, 139–40, 224; CEO and, 168; undervaluation in stock market and, 167–68

Divisionalization, 21–22, 26, 216; CEO and, 173; decision making and, 133, 135; entrepreneurial approach to, 132; growth and, 122; internal reporting system and, 123; in postwar years, 79; reorganization of, 193; structural evolution and, 144–45, 147

Donner (CEO of GM), 169

Downs, Anthony, 42

Dulles, John Foster, 182

DuPont Corporation, 8, 24, 130, 144, 150, 169–70, 204

Economica, 63

Economies of scale, 16, 69, 72, 147, 163, 192, 193

Economist, The, 31, 132, 171

Education, 99–102, 230–31, 233; occupational changes and, 111

Eisenhower, Dwight D., 23, 34, 35, 37, 40, 41, 182, 233

Employment/population (E/P) ratio, 96–97

Engineers, 103–5

Entrepreneurship: CEOs and, 177; divisional, 132; financial markets and, 225–26; in high-technology industries, 90; Knight on, 60–61; Marshall on, 58; scale and, 65, 71; Schumpeter on, 64–65; Smith on, 57

European Economic Community (EEC), 81, 86

Exxon, 8, 24, 127, 138; 1983 *Annual Report*, 89, 126

Fackenthal, Frank, 40

Farming, *see* Agriculture

Financial management, criteria of, 170–71

Financial markets, 11, 223–26

Financier (Reich), 87

Firestone Tire and Rubber, 74

Forbes, 8

Ford, Henry, II, 47

Ford Foundation, 47

Ford Motor Company, 74, 166

Fortune, 8, 17, 126–29, 131, 142, 145

Fortune 500 companies, 68, 141, 142, 172

Foundations, 46–49, 52

France, 83, 105

Friedman, Milton, 149

Functions of the Executive (Barnard), 64

Further Up the Organization (Townsend), 14, 195

Galbraith, John Kenneth, 65, 67–68, 71

Geneen, Harold, 87, 224

General Electric, 8, 22, 74, 90, 130, 170, 175

General Motors, 74, 144, 153, 166, 169, 228

Germany, 105; nineteenth-century, 59; *see also* West Germany

Gerstenberg (CEO of GM), 169

Getty Petroleum, 190

GI Bill, 79, 107

Goodyear Tire and Rubber Company, 74

Government agencies, 42–46, 52, 54

Government contracts, 89–91

Grace, J. Peter, 44

Graham, Katharine, 142

Index

Index

R. J. Reynolds, 224
RCA, 14–15, 23, 130; *Annual Report—1983*, 215
Reagan, Ronald, 44, 53, 228
Recession, 11, 129, 190; divestitures during, 14
Recruitment, 42, 156–57; by Catholic Church, 31; changes in, 201–2; in postwar years, 80
Reich, Cary, 87
Reinhardt, Uwe, 175
Reliance Electric, 127
Republic Steel, 226
Research and development (R & D), 91; board of directors and, 183–84; federal funds for, 89, 90; investments in, 218; management of, 129–32, 204; in matrix system, 145, 146; public investment in, 230; scientists and engineers employed in, 104; universities and, 42
Responsibility: in Catholic Church, 30; of CEO, 22–23, 25, 165, 167–79; delegation of, 19, 21, 217; diffusion of, 154, 163; reorganization of, 193
Retirement, 97; early, 190
Riboud, Jean, 131, 180
Robert Wood Johnson Foundation, 48
Roosevelt, Franklin D., 33, 53, 63, 75, 76, 182, 214
Roosevelt, Theodore, 228
Royal Dutch/Shell, 207

Sarnoff, David, 130
Scale, 6, 26, 29, 52–55; of Catholic Church, 31; challenges of, 119–20; of conglomerates, 88; decision making and, 11; economies of, 16, 69, 72, 147, 163, 192, 193; entrepreneurship and, 57, 65, 71; human resources and, 71–72, 200; impact on decision making of, 133–36; of military, 36, 38; organizational structure and, 71; specialization based on, 60; of universities, 40, 41; vulnerability and, 220; *see also* Growth
Schlumberger, 152, 180, 207
Schmidt, Benno, 180
Schumpeter, Joseph, 64–65, 67, 69, 71

Scientific American, ix
Scientific personnel, 102–8; management and, 130–31
Sears, Roebuck & Company, 144, 196
Securities and Exchange Commission (SEC), 125
Service industries, percentage of population employed in, 109–12
Services: The New Economy (Stanback), ix
Services of Supply, 32
Sherman Anti-Trust Act (1890), 61
Silicon Valley (California), 90
Simon, Herbert, 65–66, 70, 71
Singapore, 84
Skandinaviska Enskilda Bank, 184
Small business enterprises, 191; competition from, 219
Smith, Adam, 56–57, 62, 70
Smith, Roger B., 153
Sociopolitical environment, 227–34
Sohio, 127
Somervell, Brehon B., 32–33
South Africa, 176
South Korea, 83
Sovern, Michael I., 40
Spain, 84
Staff, 147; CEO and, 179–81
Stakeholders, 149
Stalin, Josef, 74
Stanback, Thomas, Jr., ix
Standard Oil, 8
Stanford University, 105
State, U.S. Department of, 175
Statistical Abstract of the United States, 1982–83, 106
Steel industry, 129, 178, 213
Stimson, Henry L., 33
Stock ownership, 61, 63; financial markets and, 224; internal corporate reporting and, 124
Supreme Headquarters Allied Powers Europe (SHAPE), 40
Sweden, 83, 84, 184
Swift Meatpacking Company, 8
Switzerland, 145

Taiwan, 83, 84
Takeovers, unfriendly, 177–78

241